Historical Sources in U.S. Reading Education 1900–1970

An Annotated Bibliography

Richard D. Robinson

University of Missouri–Columbia

Columbia, Missouri, USA

Editor

INTERNATIONAL

Reading Association

800 Barksdale Road, PO Box 8139
Newark, Delaware 19714-8139, USA
www.reading.org

The International Reading Association attempts, through its publications, to provide a forum for a wide spectrum of opinions on reading. This policy permits divergent viewpoints without implying the endorsement of the Association.

Director of Publications   Joan M. Irwin
Editor in Chief, Books   Matthew W. Baker
Permissions Editor   Janet S. Parrack
Associate Editor   Tori Mello
Publications Coordinator   Beth Doughty
Association Editor   David K. Roberts
Production Department Manager   Iona Sauscermen
Art Director   Boni Nash
Senior Electronic Publishing Specialist   Anette Schütz-Ruff
Electronic Publishing Specialist   Cheryl J. Strum
Electronic Publishing Assistant   Jeanine K. McGann

Project Editor   Matthew W. Baker

Library of Congress Cataloging-in-Publication Data

   Historical sources in U.S. reading education, 1900–1970 : an annotated bibliography / Richard D. Robinson, editor.
       p.   cm.
   Includes index.
   ISBN 0-87207-271-1
   1. Reading—United States—Abstracts.   2. Reading—United States—Bibliography.   I. Robinson, Richard David, 1940–
LB1050.H57   2000   00-025445
016.4284'07—dc21

Contents

ACKNOWLEDGMENTS

The author wishes to acknowledge the help and support of members of the History of Special Interest Group of the International Reading Association in the development of this publication. I especially thank Dr. Jennifer Monaghan of The Brooklyn College of the City University of New York, for her valuable input throughout this project.

INTRODUCTION

The Importance
of the History of Reading
for Today's Classroom Teacher

It [reading] is the noblest of arts, the medium by which there still comes to us the loftiest inspirations, the highest ideals, the purest feelings, that have been allowed mankind.... Reading as a psycho-physiological process is almost as good as a miracle.

Edmund Huey
The Psychology and Pedagogy of Reading, 1908

For a people to be without history, or to be ignorant of its history, is for a man to be without his country—condemned forever to make the same discoveries that have been made in the past, invent the same techniques, wrestle with the same problems, commit the same errors, and condemned, too, to forfeit the rich pleasures of recollection.

Henry Steel Commager
The Nature and Study of History, 1965

The teaching of reading today is based on a rich historical legacy of the past. Many of the same reading issues facing modern classroom teachers also were of concern to former educators. In studying this history it is clear that these teachers of the past often thought deeply and in many cases insightfully about the reading process. Although conditions frequently differed from today in terms of teaching methods and materials, there are still threads or themes that have been evident in reading education from the earliest days (Robinson, 1989; Robinson, Baker, & Clegg, 1998). Note the following quotes from reading teachers of the past and compare their thoughts with current issues and trends in reading education.

A teacher writing in the year 1714 concerning his philosophy regarding language development in young children makes this rather interesting comment:

> It is certain that many [students] become authors before they have been readers.... (Steele, 1714, p. 279)

Also note this definition of reading from an even earlier period:

> Reading or language is the outward expression of the mind. (Warblis, 1646, p. 1)

Consider another teacher's reading philosophy:

> When a child can talk, 'tis time he should learn to read. And when he reads, put into his hands some very pleasant book suited to his capacity, wherein the entertainment he finds may draw him in, and reward his pains in reading. Aesop's fables with pictures may be made use of to this purpose. Talk often to him about the stories he has just read, and hear him tell them. This will bring him to delight in reading and to express himself handsomely. (Waugh, 1752, pp. 11–12)

What did language teachers of the past believe about the organization of instruction? Here are two alternatives that were considered:

> If three or four persons agree to read the same book, and each bring his own remarks upon it, at some set hours appointed for conversation, and they communicate mutually their sentiments on the subject, and debate about it in a friendly manner, this practice will render the reading of any author more abundantly beneficial to every one of them. (Watts, 1811, p. 43)

If several persons engaged in the same study take into their hands distinct treatises on one subject, and appoint a season of communication once a week, they may inform each other in a brief manner concerning the sense, sentiments, and method of those several authors, and thereby promote each other's improvement, either by recommending the perusal of the same book to their companions, or perhaps by satisfying their inquiries concerning it by conversation, without everyone's perusing it. (Watts, 1811, p. 44)

Also, what about the use of meaningless activities in the teaching of reading?

To teach reading as a mere combination of words which do not teach anything, which are often unintelligible to young persons and which leave minds in states of listless curiosity and total ignorance is a waste of time. (Blair, 1806, p. 10)

This is only a small sample of educators from the past talking about reading, often in a surprisingly modern vein. To know this legacy is to enhance our current professional experiences as reading teachers through the rich heritage we have inherited. Consider this final comment:

We need to feel kinship with the people we study, for this is exactly what engages our interest and makes us feel connected. We come to see ourselves as inheritors of a tradition that provides a sound mooring and some security against the transience of the modern world. (Wineburg, 1999)

References

Blair, D. (1806). *The class book of three hundred and sixty-five reading lessons, adapted to the use of schools for every day in the year*. London: R. Taylor.

Commager, H.S. (1965). *The nature and study of history*. Columbus, OH: Merrill.

Robinson, R.D. (1989). Reading teachers of the past—What they believed about reading. *Reading Improvement, 26*, 231–238.

Robinson, R.D., Baker, E., & Clegg, L. (1998). Literacy and the pendulum of change: Lessons for the 21st century. *Peabody Journal of Education, 73*, 15–30.

Steele, R. (1714). *The reader*. London: R. Tonfon.

Warblis, S. (1646). *A common writing: Whereby two, although not understanding one of the others language, yet by the helps thereof, may communicate their minds one to another.* London: n.p.

Watts, I. (1811). *The improvement of the mind.* London: F.C. and J. Rivington.

Waugh, J. (1752). *Education of children and young students in all its branches with a short catalogue of the best books in polite learning and the sciences.* London: Waugh.

Wineburg, S. (1999). Historical thinking and other unnatural acts. *Phi Delta Kappan, 80*(7), 488–499.

SELECTION PROCESS

In an article on selecting literacy research that had made a difference, Shanahan and Neuman (1997) describe the difficulties often inherent in the selection process. They note that final decisions as to what to include or not include in a collection of this type should be made using many factors. For instance, in the selection process for this bibliography, not only were works selected based on their individual contribution to reading education, but also because of their historical importance and influence on other work as well. In numerous cases the final selection was an arbitrary one that easily could have changed to include different resources. This book includes those works that were felt to be of the greatest use to those interested in the history of reading. In general, the following criteria were used:

The impact of the source on the field of reading education.

The extent and usefulness of the source's bibliography as a guide to related research.

The implications of the source for current practice.

The importance of the source as a contribution to the study of the field of literacy history.

What follows are the results of this selection process. No attempt has been made to include every possible resource, but rather the selections were made to enable readers to begin their own work in the study of the history of reading. The references here are predominately from the period 1900 to 1970, but there are a number of publications included that fall beyond this period. In most instances, especially with the more recent references, they were included because of their important discussions of past reading research and practices.

Reference

Shanahan, T., & Neuman, S.B. (1997). Conversations: Literacy research that makes a difference. *Reading Research Quarterly, 32,* 202–210.

SECTION ONE
General Works in Reading

Of making books there is no end....

Ecclesiastes, 12:12

Reading maketh a full man, conference a ready man, and writing an exact man.

Francis Bacon
Of Studies, 1625

Included in this section are a variety of references that reflect the wide spectrum of interest in the field of reading. These range from works by authors who view reading purely from a historical perspective to those who write about reading as personal experience with print. In most cases, each of these examples represents a large genre of related books and other materials.

ADLER, M.J. (1940). *How to read a book: The art of getting a liberal education*. New York: Simon & Schuster.

> This volume is a well-known example of a group of books on the topic of reading. Writing for the general public, Adler notes that there is an "art" to reading that extends far beyond just mechanics. The book includes chapters titled "The Reading of 'Reading,'" "The Great Books," and "Free Minds and Free Men." This is an important book in that it describes the purposes of reading as a

lifetime activity. An interesting companion volume is *The New Lifetime Reading Plan* (Fadiman, 1960).

AUSTIN, M.C., & MORRISON, C. (1961). *The torch lighters: Tomorrow's teachers of reading*. Cambridge, MA: Harvard University, Graduate School of Education.

> The professional training of classroom teachers is a major focus of this report. The results indicate that teacher education programs at the time were not adequately preparing future reading teachers. This study was an important influence on the development and change of teacher preparation programs.

AUSTIN, M.C., & MORRISON, C. (1963). *The first R: The Harvard report on reading in elementary schools*. New York: Macmillan.

> This book reports on various aspects of elementary school reading programs, based on a study of 1,000 school systems. Topics include the components of the reading program, special services, professional growth of teachers, and the role of the school administrator. This is an invaluable resource for reading researchers interested in the problems and possible solutions of schoolwide reading programs. (See the previous reference for Austin & Morrison, 1961, for a related discussion.)

BURY, R. DE (1948). *The philobiblon* (The love of books). Berkeley and Los Angeles: University of California. (Original work published 1345)

> *The Philobiblon* is one of those special books that has become an almost official handbook for bibliophiles. Recognized widely as the first book on the love of reading, this volume represents a growing area in the study of the book. Note the titles of some of the chapters: "What Benefits the Love of Books Confer"; "What Love is Reasonably Due Books"; and for reading educators, "Of the Manner of Distributing Our Books to All Students." *The Philobiblon* reads as if it were written yesterday, with every page revealing the author's deep love for language and reading.

CRANNEY, A.G., & MILLER, J. (1987). History of reading: Status and sources of a growing field. *Journal of Reading, 30*, 388–398.

> An important article on various aspects of the study of the history of reading. This discussion notes the current status of this field both in terms of its support in the academic community as well as the types of courses being taught in the history of reading. Of particular note for researchers is the extensive annotated bibliography.

DAVIDSON, C.N. (1989). *Reading in America: Literature and social history*. Baltimore: Johns Hopkins University Press.

> This collection of lessons is an excellent introduction to the history of the book. Chapters include discussions on early reading materials such as chapbooks, gender issues as they relate to literacy instruction in colonial New England, and literacy and the mass media.

HARRIS, W.V. (1989). *Ancient literacy*. Cambridge, MA: Harvard University Press.

> This is a scholarly discussion of reading in the ancient Greek and Roman empires. A noteworthy feature for reading researchers is the extensive bibliography of references related to reading and writing in the ancient world.

HENRICKSON, G.L. (1929). Ancient reading. *The Classical Journal, 25*, 182–196.

> A historical description of reading in antiquity, centering on the Greek and Roman empires. This is an important resource for those studying the early history of reading training.

HUEY, E. (1908). *Psychology and pedagogy of reading*. New York: Macmillan. (Reprinted in 1968 by The MIT Press, Cambridge, MA)

> This book is considered one of the classic references in reading education. Many of the issues Huey addresses, such as the relationship between inner speech and silent reading, are still being debated today. Of particular importance in this book is the ex-

tensive bibliography with its emphasis on early eye-movement experimentation. For further study on this topic, the following references are suggested:

Dearborn, W.F. (1906). *The psychology of reading: An experimental study of the reading process and eye-movements*. New York: Science Press.

Dodge, R. (1907). An experimental study of visual fixation. *Psychological Review Monograph Supplements, VIII*(4).

Javal, E. (1879). Essai sur la physiologie de la lecture. *Annales dí Oculistique, 82*, 242–253.

JERROLDS, B.W. (1977). *Reading reflections: The history of the International Reading Association*. Newark, DE: International Reading Association.

This volume is an important historical statement of the development of the International Reading Association (IRA) from its beginning through 1977. Of particular importance to reading researchers are the many interviews with former IRA presidents and board members. Also helpful are the detailed appendixes that contain information on the reading organizations that merged to form what became the International Reading Association.

KAESTLE, C.F. (1990). Introduction. *History of Education Quarterly* (Special issue on the history of literacy), *30*, 487–491.

Reading education developments in a number of international settings such as England, Japan, Scotland, Spain, and Wales are discussed in this issue. For those who wish to compare and contrast national programs of reading instruction, this is an important reference.

KAESTLE, C.F., MOORE, H.D., STEDMAN, C., TINSLEY, K., & TOLLINGER, W.V. (1991). *Literacy in the United States: Readers and reading since 1880*. New Haven, CT: Yale University Press.

This book is unusual in the field of historical reading research in that it not only reports on the historical development of reading from 1880 to date but also provides a rich and detailed interpretation of these reading activities. The book defines the terms *reading* and *illiteracy* and addresses the question, What were the specific behaviors of readers during a particular time period? in the context of the social conditions at the time. For those interested in the effects of reading on various U.S. social practices, this is an important resource.

KERFOOT, J.B. (1916). *How to read.* Boston: Houghton Mifflin.

A general discussion of the ways in which people have learned to read and the reasons they read. This is an important historical reference for its extended discussion of reading as a means of individual self-improvement. (See Porter, 1870, in this section for an earlier discussion of related material.)

LARRICK, N. (1965, September 11). The all white world of children's books. *Saturday Review, 48,* 63–65, 84–85.

The author surveyed more than 5,000 children's books published during the years 1962–1964 and found that only 6.7% of them portrayed African Americans and less than 1% told of African Americans during this time period. This article was one of the first to identify multicultural issues, and following the article's publication, there was an increased interest in multicultural education.

MANGUEL, A. (1996). *A history of reading.* New York: Viking.

This book is a personal history of the author's many and varied encounters with print, which he then uses as an introduction to the study of the history of reading. Although this book was written for a broader audience, it does provide a good overview of the history of reading instruction.

MATTHEWS, M.M. (1966). *Teaching to read: Historically considered.* Chicago: University of Chicago Press.

This book is an important reference in the study of the historical past in literacy education. In a general format the author traces language development from the earliest times through the early 1960s. Of particular interest is the bibliography that provides a good overview of the study of the history of reading. Although more in-depth resources have followed this publication, it is recommended that reading researchers who are relatively new to the field begin with this historical discussion of reading developments of the past.

MONAGHAN, E.J. (1988). Literacy instruction and gender in colonial New England. *American Quarterly, 40,* 18–41.

A detailed discussion of the teaching of reading skills in colonial America. This insightful article includes descriptions of what parts of society were instructed in various reading skills as well as what methods were used. The influences of religion, politics, and economics are detailed as to their effect on various aspects of language instruction. Of particular importance is the author's discussion of several continuing research problems associated with historical reading research, such as evaluating literacy levels based solely on the ability of individuals to correctly sign their names.

MONAGHAN, E.J., & SAUL, E.W. (1987). The reader, the scribe, the thinker: A critical look at the history of American reading and writing instruction. In T.S. Popkewitz (Ed.), *The formation of school subjects: The struggle for creating an American institution* (pp. 85–122). Philadelphia: Falmer.

This essay discusses the historical background related to the teaching of reading and writing, noting the disparity in favor of reading education for much of this period. Both social and political reasons for this dominance of reading instruction are discussed. The recent increased interest in writing at all levels also is documented.

MOORE, D.W., MONAGHAN, E.J., & HARTMAN, D.K. (1997). Values of literacy history. *Reading Research Quarterly, 32,* 90–102.

An enlightening discussion of the values of the study of literacy history by three noted language historians. The authors address many of the vital questions in this discipline, both in individual statements and in dialogue with one another. This article contains an outstanding list of related references on the topic of the study of historical reading.

MOORE, D.W., READENCE, J.E., & RICKELMAN, R.J. (1983). An historical exploration of content area reading instruction. *Reading Research Quarterly, 18*, 419–438.

This article is a historical discussion of the factors that predominantly shaped the teaching of content reading during the early part of the 20th century. Of particular note in the development of content reading is the influence of educational philosophers including humanists, developmentists, and scientific determinists. The authors identify five issues relevant to the historical development of content reading: (1) locus of instruction, (2) reading demands of various subjects, (3) study, (4) reading materials, and (5) age focus. This article also contains an excellent bibliography.

OLMERT, M. (1992). *The Smithsonian book of books*. New York: Random House.

This book is representative of a growing genre today on the topic of "the book." Chapter titles include "Scrolls and Scribes," "Illuminating the Dark Ages," "The Gutenberg Revolution," and "Bookmaker's Craft." This is an excellent introduction to the study of the many facets of the book as both a means of communication as well as an art object.

PORTER, N. (1870). *Books and reading or what books shall I read or how should I read them*. New York: Charles Scribner and Sons.

This book is a scholarly and wide-ranging discussion of the world of literature and reading by the then president of Yale University. Of particular note in this reference is the extensive bibliography of suggested readings in a wide variety of content areas. These include materials from history, science, geography, and language. This book is an invaluable reference for those studying the reading habits and interests of people in the 19th century. There also is a very complete index of cited references, which is somewhat of a rarity in books of this age and type.

ROBINSON, R.D. (1989). Reading teachers of the past—What they believed about reading. *Reading Improvement, 26,* 231–238.

This article details the opinions of reading teachers of the past, from as early as 1660, concerning their definitions of reading, classroom goals, organization of reading instruction, and ways of dealing with problem readers.

SAENGER, P. (1997). *Space between words: The origins of silent reading.* Stanford, CA: Stanford University Press.

This scholarly book is a discussion of the influence of word separation as being a vital element in the development of silent reading during medieval times. This is a vital resource for those interested in early developments in the use of silent reading. Of particular importance to reading researchers is the extensive glossary and reference sections of this book.

VYGOTSKY, L.S. (1962). *Thought and language.* (E. Hanfmann & G. Vakar, Trans.). Cambridge, MA: The MIT Press. (Original work published 1934)

Of particular interest to Vygotsky in this work is the fact that language is both highly personal and at the same time social as well. This relationship between the individual and society in terms of language development is at the center of Vygotsky's work. For those who wish to study the primary writings of this influential language theorist, this is an important work.

VYGOTSKY, L.S. (1978). *Mind in society. The development of higher psychological processes.* (M. Cole, V. John-Steiner, S. Scribner, & E. Souberman, Eds. and Trans.). Cambridge, MA: Harvard University Press. (Original work published 1934)

The study of Lev Vygotsky's work, as it relates to children's thought and language, has had a significant influence on many aspects of school curriculum and practice today. The editors have translated Vygotsky's original writing and have carefully edited these primary references into two general categories: Basic Theory and Data, and Educational Implications. Although many consider Vygotsky's work *Thought and Language* (see the preceding reference), as the primary expression of his educational ideas, this book clearly shows that the scope of his work and study extends far beyond this basic reference. Of particular note for educational researchers is the listing of Vygotsky's publications during the period 1915 to 1935, including those published in English.

WOOD, E. (1963). Speed reading. *NEA Journal, 52,* 44–46.

The impact of speed reading on the general public was, at one time, immense. This influence was shown clearly in the development of speed reading machines, courses of study, and related activities. This article is an early example of the writing of a prominent figure in the speed reading movement.

SECTION TWO
Summaries of Reading Research

Books are the legacies that a great genius leaves to mankind, which are delivered down from generation to generation, as presents to the posterity of those who are yet to be born.

Joseph Addison
Spectator, 1711–1712

This section contains summaries of reading research and study. For those interested in the rich history of reading, these volumes represent an invaluable resource for related study and investigation. Although works by William S. Gray, such as his yearly *Summary of Investigations Relating to Reading*, are relatively well known, there are other works that are often less recognized and yet have great value. For instance, the summaries of reading research by Emmett Betts (1934, 1945) and the work of Ruth Strang (1939) represent major contributions to the study of important research done in the early history of reading. Also included in this section are reviews of the three volumes of the *Handbook of Reading Research* (Pearson, Barr, Kamil, & Mosenthal, 1984; Barr, Kamil, Mosenthal, & Pearson, 1991; Kamil, Mosenthal, Pearson, & Barr, 2000), which represent the current thinking of the time in many aspects of reading education.

BARR, R., KAMIL, M.L., MOSENTHAL, P., & PEARSON, P.D. (1991). *Handbook of reading research: Volume II*. White Plains, NY: Longman.

This reference continues the work started in Volume I (see Pearson et al., 1984, in this section). Over 30 reading topics are reviewed under the following four sections: "Society and Literacy," "Task and Format Variables in Reading Research," "Constructs of Reader Process," and "Literacy and Schooling." Extensive bibliographies accompany each of the chapter contributions.

BETTS, E.A. (1934). *Bibliography on the problems related to the analysis, prevention, and correction of reading difficulties.* Meadville, PA: Keystone View Company.

This reference, along with Betts and Betts (1945) (see the entry that follows), make up one of the most complete records of past reading study. This particular bibliography describes almost 1,200 historical studies on the diagnosis and remediation of reading disabilities.

BETTS, E.A., & BETTS, T.M. (1945). *An index to professional literature on reading and related topics.* New York: American Book.

For researchers studying the history of reading this is one of the most important resources available. The authors reference over 8,200 articles, books, and other studies in the field of reading from 1880 to 1945. Of particular help to the researcher is the complete topical index included. For instance, there are more than 200 references on comprehension, 800 on instructional procedures, and an equal number related to remedial and corrective reading. Historically interesting topics such as kinesthetic techniques, dominance factors, strephosymbolia, and typography concerns reflect the changing issues and trends in the field of reading education.

BROOKS, G., PUGH, A.K., & HALL, N. (1993). *Further studies in the history of reading.* Cheshire, UK: United Kingdom Reading Association.

This resource contains an important series of papers on the history of reading instruction. Of particular importance in this book are the questions asked about current research in historical literacy as well as suggestions for further research in this area.

GRAY, W.S. (1925). *Summary of investigations relating to reading* (Supplemental Educational Monographs, No. 28). Chicago: University of Chicago Press.

> This is the first in a series of reviews of reading research, which are some of the most valuable resources in the early history of reading education. The first issue in this series is of particular importance because of its succinct review of the early history of reading. It includes 436 annotated references beginning in the 1880s.

GRAY, W.S., & OTHERS. (various dates from 1926 to 1997). *Summary of investigations relating to reading.*

> This general title was used in a continuing series of annual summaries of reading research and related studies for 50 years. From 1926 through 1932, under the editorial leadership of William S. Gray, this summary of reading research was published in the *The Elementary School Journal.* From 1933 through 1960, annual summaries edited by Gray appeared in the *Journal of Educational Research.* Helen Robinson assumed the editorship of the Annual Summary following Gray's death in 1960, and for the years 1961 to 1964 this research review appeared in *The Reading Teacher.* Beginning in 1965 and extending through 1978, the Annual Summary was published as a single issue of *Reading Research Quarterly* with Helen Robinson as editor during the period 1965 to 1969. In 1970 Sam Weintraub began his long association with the *Annual Summary.* His tenure as editor lasted from this time until the last issue of the *Annual Summary of Investigations Relating to Reading* was published in 1997. This report was published by the International Reading Association as a separate publication from 1978 through 1997. Taken in total, the *Annual Summary* represents the most complete and readily accessible catalog of resources in the field of reading.

KAMIL, M.L., MOSENTHAL, P., PEARSON, P.D., & BARR, R. (2000). *Handbook of reading research: Volume III.* Mahwah, NJ: Erlbaum.

> The contents of this volume are divided into the following four sections: "Literacy Research Around the World," "Methods of Lit-

eracy Research," "Literacy Processes," and "Literacy Policies." Each chapter includes comprehensive reviews of relevant reading research. The three volumes in this series (see also Barr et al., 1991; Pearson et al., 1984) are of invaluable help to reading researchers.

PEARSON, P.D., BARR, R., KAMIL, M.L., & MOSENTHAL, P. (1984). *Handbook of reading research*: New York: Longman.

This reference along with Volume II and Volume III of this series (see Barr et al., 1991, and Kamil et al., 2000, in this section) constitutes one of the most complete references of research in reading education. The materials in this volume are divided into three sections: "Methodological Issues," "Basic Processes: The State of the Art," and "Instructional Practices: The State of the Art." Each of the 25 chapters provides a critical overview of an area of reading with an extensive accompanying bibliography. For those interested in reading from a historical perspective, of particular note is the chapter by Richard L. Venezky titled "The History of Reading Research" (pp. 3–38).

SMITH, N.B. (1966). Reading: Seventy-five years of progress. In H.A. Robinson (Ed.), *Reading: Seventy-five years of progress* (Proceedings of the annual conference on reading held at the University of Chicago, 1966, pp. 3–12). Chicago: University of Chicago Press.

This article, by one of the noted historians of reading, is a review of the previous 75 years of reading development. It is the theme article in the culminating edition of a series of noteworthy reading yearbooks from the University of Chicago issued from 1939 through 1966 (see the review of these Yearbooks in this section). Of particular note for reading researchers is the comprehensive bibliography.

STAHL, N.A., & KING, J.R. (2000). A history of college reading. In R.A. Flippo & D.C. Caverly (Eds.), *Handbook of College Reading and Study Research* (1–23). Mahwah, NJ: Erlbaum.

An extensive review of the history of college reading instruction with particular emphasis on the primary resources needed to do research in this area. Of particular note to literacy researchers is the detailed discussion of the philosophy of historical literacy investigations as well as information on the effective use of appropriate methods for the collection of this type of data.

STRANG, R. (1939). *Bibliography relating to reading on the high school and college level.* New York: Bureau of Publications, Teachers College, Columbia University.

This bibliography is a major resource for researchers working in the fields of high school, college, and adult reading. The title is somewhat misleading in that the more than 1,500 references, while emphasizing older readers, also include some studies concerned with younger children. A sampling of the topics covered in this reference include perception and eye-movements, reading in the content areas, case studies of reading difficulties, and related bibliographies.

SUMMERS, E.D. (Ed.). (1969). *20 year annotated index to* The Reading Teacher. Newark, DE: International Reading Association.

This volume provides an annotated review of 816 articles from the first 20 years of *The Reading Teacher.* Of particular help to the literacy researcher is the classification of these references into 18 major categories, arranged according to year of publication.

TRAXLER, A.E. (various dates). *Research in reading.* New York: Educational Records Bureau.

This series of reviews of reading research was published from 1941 to 1957 under various titles. Of particular note in these publications are the insightful annotations provided for each reference. Also included in each volume is an index of authors and topics. Specific titles include the following:

Traxler, A.E. (1941). *Ten years of research in reading* (No. 32). New York: Educational Records Bureau.

The author reviews a total of 618 studies from the period January 1, 1930 through January 1, 1940.

Traxler, A.E. (1946). *Another five years of research in reading* (No. 46). New York: Educational Records Bureau.

The author reviews a total of 527 studies from the period January 1, 1940 through January 1, 1945.

Traxler, A.E. (1955). *Eight more years of research in reading* (No. 64). New York: Educational Records Bureau.

The author reviews a total of 760 studies from the period January, 1, 1945 through July 1, 1953.

Traxler, A.E. (1960). *Research in reading during another four years* (No. 75). New York: Educational Records Bureau.

The author reviews a total of 438 studies from the period July 1953 through December 31, 1957.

A separate series of three bibliographies related to the diagnosis and remediation of reading problems also were published under the direction of Arthur Traxler. They also were annotated and indexed. Specific volumes in this series include the following:

Traxler, A.E. (1937). Summary and selected bibliography of research relating to the diagnosis and teaching of reading, 1930–1937 (Supplementary Bulletin A). New York: Educational Records Bureau.

The author reviews a total of 283 studies from the period January 1, 1930 through September 30, 1937.

Traxler, A.E., & Seder, M. (1938). Summary and selected bibliography of research relating to the diagnosis and teaching of reading, October 1937 to September 1938 (Supplementary Bulletin C). New York: Educational Records Bureau.

The authors review a total of 65 studies from the period October 1, 1937 through September 30, 1938.

Traxler, A.E., & Seder, M. (1939). Summary and selected bibliography of research relating to the diagnosis and teaching of reading, October 1938 to September 1939. (Supplementary Bulletin F). New York: Educational Records Bureau.

The authors review a total of 114 studies from the period October 1, 1938 through September 30, 1939.

SECTION THREE

Reading Paradigms, Perception, and Word Recognition

[There is] growing agreement that there is no one and only ortho-
dox way of teaching and learning this greatest and hardest of all
arts [reading].

G. Stanley Hall
How to Teach Reading and What to Read in School, 1887

It can hardly be doubted therefore that a child would learn to
name 26 unfamiliar words sooner than the unknown, unheard-
of and unthought of letters of the alphabet.

Horace Mann
Annual Reports of the Secretary of the Board of Education
of Massachusetts for 1837/1838

Reading strategies have long been a source of intense interest
to the reading community. Although many different approaches
have been developed, perhaps the two most dominant strategies of the 20th century could be categorized as being "whole
word" and "whole language." This section includes references to
these paradigms as well as several others that have been used
with varying degrees of success. It should be noted that the arbitrary ending date of this publication precludes most of the whole
language research and discussion that came later than 1970.

Additionally in this section is a wide variety of philosophical and practical approaches to the role of perception and word recognition in the reading process. Of particular note, as reflected in some of the works in this section, is the continuing debate in the reading community related to the issue of phonics and its appropriate place in an effective reading program. Also included in this section are a number of references to eye movement research as this work relates to reading perception (see Anderson & Dearborn, 1952; Rayner, 1997).

ADAMS, M.J. (1990). *Beginning to read.* Cambridge, MA: The MIT Press.

> This is an important book in the continuing debate about the role of phonics and its place in reading instruction. The book has been considered by most reading authorities to be an equitable discussion of this controversial subject.

ANDERSON, I.H., & DEARBORN, W.F. (1952). *The psychology of teaching reading.* New York: The Roland Press.

> This is an important volume in the study of the history of reading instruction because of its extensive discussion of early leaders in this area; e.g., Cattell, Javal, and Dearborn. Of particular usefulness to reading researchers is the extensive bibliography of 368 references.

ARTLEY, A.S. (1953). *Your child learns to read.* Chicago: Scott Foresman.

> An extended explanation of the effective use of the basal reader, especially as it relates to the whole word philosophy of reading instruction. This is an important resource for those interested in a publisher's perspective of this philosophy.

AUKERMAN, R.C. (1971). *Approaches to beginning reading.* New York: John Wiley & Sons.

> This reference reviews more than 100 approaches to the teaching of reading, dividing these various methods into 10 major cate-

gories. The scope of this review of reading practices includes both common approaches as well as more obscure ones. This reference is an excellent source for those interested in the various reading methods that have been used in the past. (For information on more recent developments in the area of reading strategies consult Tierney, Readence, & Dishner, 1980, which is reviewed in this section.)

BALMUTH, M. (1982). *The roots of phonics: A historical introduction.* New York: McGraw-Hill.

This scholarly reference, as noted by one reviewer, is of "inestimable value" in the study of phonics from an historical perspective. The author traces the history of phonics through four strands: writing systems in general, the English writing system, spoken English, and English spelling patterns. For those interested in the role phonics has played historically in reading education, this is a definitive resource.

CHALL, J.S. (1967). *Learning to read: The great debate.* New York: McGraw-Hill.

This book is often referred to as a landmark study of the "phonics question." Chall's work has had an important influence on classroom teachers' attitudes and instructional methods as they apply to the role of phonics in an effective reading program.

CLYMER, T. (1963). The utility of phonics generalizations in the primary grades. *The Reading Teacher, 16,* 252–258.

A landmark study of the usefulness of the most often-taught phonics generalizations. The general conclusions of this research indicate that the utility of many phonics generalizations is of limited value because there were often numerous exceptions in the author's study.

COLE, L. (1938). *The improvement of reading.* New York: Farrar & Rinehart.

This book is an early explanation of what was to become the whole word approach to the teaching of reading. This volume is a valuable resource for those interested in an early description of this approach in the classroom setting.

DOWNING, J.A. (1962). *The initial teaching alphabet.* New York: Macmillian.

> The use of the initial teaching alphabet (i.t.a.) was based on the idea that young readers would benefit most from materials that were written based on the sounds of English rather traditional orthography in their first experience being read to. After a period of time using i.t.a., readers then would transfer to traditionally spelled text materials. One of the benefits of i.t.a. noted by the authors was that students trained in this method tended to be better writers. For further information related to i.t.a. see the following:

> > Downing, J.A. (1964). *The initial teaching alphabet reading experiment.* London: Evans Brothers for the University of London Institute of Education.

> > Pitman, J. (1960). *Learning to read.* London: Royal Society of Arts

> > Pitman, J. (1969). *Alphabets and reading: The initial teaching alphabet.* New York: Pitman.

GOODMAN, K. (1967). Reading: A psycholinguistic guessing game. *Journal of the Reading Specialist, 6,* 126–135.

> Considered by many to be a classic in the reading field, this article set the stage for influential work that was to follow, especially in the early discussion of the philosophy that became whole language and the assessment of reading through the use of miscue analysis.

GRAY, W.S. (1948). *On their own in reading.* Chicago: Scott, Foresman.

> This is an important reference on the role of effective word perception by one of the pioneers in the field of reading education. This is an excellent resource for those who are interested in a basic overview of the various aspects of word analysis.

Rayner, K. (1997). Understanding eye movements in reading. *Scientific Studies of Reading, 1,* 317, 339.

> A contemporary review of studies on eye movement research. This article in connection with Anderson and Dearborn (1952) (see reference in this section) will provide a good overview of both historical and current work in this area.

Smith, F. (1971). *Understanding reading: A psycholinguistic analysis of reading and learning to read.* New York: Holt, Rinehart and Winston.

> This book is a landmark reference in the history of the teaching of reading. Of particular importance is the philosophical discussion of the reading process and how the implications of these ideas need to impact the classroom teaching of reading.

Smith, F. (1979). *Reading without nonsense.* New York: Teachers College Press. (Original work published in 1978 under the title *Reading.*)

> In this reference the author presents his philosophical perspective on the reading process with particular emphasis on the role of the classroom teacher.

Tierney, R.J., Readence, J.E., & Dishner, E.K. (1980). *Reading strategies and practices: A guide for improving reading instruction.* Needham Heights, MA: Allyn & Bacon.

> This is an important reference in the study of various approaches used in classroom reading instruction. When used in connection with Aukerman (1971), which is reviewed in this section, this work should provide a excellent overview of past reading practices. Subsequent editions of this book have been published in 1985, 1990, 1995, and 1999 under the title *Reading Strategies and Practices.*

Veatch, J. (1959). *Individualizing your reading program.* New York: I.P. Putnam's Sons.

This book details the philosophical foundations and classroom teaching procedures for what was to become the "individualizing reading" approach to reading instruction.

SECTION FOUR
Oral and Silent Reading

> The enriching and aesthetic values of oral reading should not be underestimated.
>
> *Guidebook for the* Fun With Dick and Jane Basic Primer, 1940

The particular role of oral and silent reading has long been a concern of both reading researchers and teachers. In this section are listed several historical references such as Buswell (1945), Quantz (1897), and Germane and Germane (1922), which provide a historical perspective on this topic. A continuing debate concerns the proper use of oral and silent reading, especially as these skills relate to time and emphasis in classroom instruction. Typical of many articles taking various perspectives on this issue are the ones by McDade (1944) and Rohrer (1943), which are discussed in this section.

BUSWELL, G.T. (1945). *Non-oral reading: A study of its use in the Chicago Public Schools* (Supplemental Educational Monographs, No. 60). Chicago: University of Chicago Press.

> This monograph reports the results of a study of 70,000 elementary students who over a 10-year period were taught reading by direct association between the visual symbol and meaning without oral pronunciation. The students in this study were found to read faster and more effectively than those who were exposed to extensive oral reading instruction.

GERMANE, C.E., & GERMANE, E.G. (1922). *Silent reading: A handbook for teachers.* Chicago: Row Peterson.

> This book is considered to be one of the most important early references on the teaching of oral and silent reading. It includes extensive discussions of topics such as the relationship between silent and oral reading, speed of reading, and remedial work in reading.

JUDD, C.H., & BUSWELL, C.H. (1922). *Silent reading: A study of the various types* (Supplemental Educational Monographs, No. 23). Chicago: University of Chicago Press.

> This discussion of various aspects of silent reading is often referenced by others in the field and thus established much of the research agenda related to silent reading for a number of years.

MCDADE, J.E. (1944). Examination of a recent criticism of nonoral beginning reading. *The Elementary School Journal, 44,* 343–351.

> This article is written in defense of the use of silent reading (called nonoral reading) as opposed to extensive initial oral reading for beginning readers. McDade refutes Rohrer's (see reference later in this section) support of oral reading as being a hindrance to eventual success in reading, particularly as it relates to speed and comprehension.

PINTER, R., & GILLILAND, A.R. (1916). Oral and silent reading. *Journal of Educational Psychology, 7,* 201–212.

> This article is one of the earliest discussions of the teaching of oral and silent reading. This is a particularly important work because of the research reported on the effectiveness of oral and silent reading at different grade levels as well as with high school and college students.

QUANTZ, J.O. (1897). Problems in the psychology of reading. *Psychological Review Monograph Supplements II,* 1–52. New York: Macmillan.

One of the earliest references to the teaching of oral reading and silent reading that includes a discussion of the possible negative influences of extensive initial oral reading on the eventual development of silent reading.

ROHRER, J.H. (1943). An analysis and evaluation of the non-oral method of reading instruction. *The Elementary School Journal*, 415–421.

This article supports the intensive use of initial oral reading as a foundation for effective instruction. See McDade (1944) earlier in this section for an opposing view of the role of oral reading.

SAENGER, P. (1997). *Space between words: The origins of silent reading*. Stanford, CA: Stanford University Press.

(See description of this book in Section One, "General Works in Reading.")

WHIPPLE, G.W. (ED.). (1921). *Silent reading: The twentieth yearbook of the National Society for the Study of Education, Part II*. Bloomington, IL: Public School Publishing Company.

An important early reference in the study of silent reading containing contributions from reading pioneers William S. Gray, Gerald O'Brien, and Gerald Yoakum.

SECTION FIVE

Vocabulary and Comprehension

"When I use a word," Humpty Dumpty said, in rather a scornful tone, "it means just what I choose it to mean—neither more nor less."

"The question is," said Alice, "whether you can make words mean so many different things."

"The question is," said Humpty Dumpty, "which is to be master—that's all."

Lewis Carroll
Through the Looking Glass, 1871

The study of comprehension and vocabulary is a relatively recent phenomenon in reading research (see Venezky, 1984, in Section Nine, "Reading Assessment"). Much of the early research related to comprehension was tied directly to rate of reading. Vocabulary studies tended to involve the identification of lists of commonly used words.

CLIFFORD, G.J. (1978). Words for schools: The applications in education of the vocabulary of Edward L. Thorndike. In P. Suppes (Ed.), *Impact of research on education: Some case studies*. Washington, DC: National Academy of Education.

The work discusses the important effect Thorndike's vocabulary research has had on classroom instruction as well as its impact on the publishing industry.

DOLCH, E.W. (1936). A basic sight vocabulary. *The Elementary School Journal, 36*, 456–460.

>This reference presents a basic sight vocabulary of 220 words common to three other word lists (International Kindergarten, the Gates, and the Wheeler-Howle). This basic sight word list shaped much of the vocabulary study and research for many years.

HILLIARD, G.E. (1924). Probable types of difficulties underlying low scores in comprehension tests. *University of Iowa Studies in Education, II*(6). Iowa City, IA: University of Iowa.

>This monograph reports the results of a survey of the existing literature on comprehension, identifying 12 factors that seem to affect this one aspect of reading. This is an important study because of its extended discussion of the then current thinking related to comprehension.

QUANTZ, J.O. (1897). Problems in the psychology of reading. *Psychological Review Monograph Supplements, II*. New York: Macmillan.

>See description in Section Four, "Oral and Silent Reading."

ROBINSON, H.A., FARAONE, V., HITTLEMAN, D.R., & UNRUH, E. (1990). *Reading comprehension instruction 1783–1987: A review of trends and research.* Newark, DE: International Reading Association.

>This book could be considered two books in one. The first book is a discussion of reading comprehension instruction between the years 1783 and 1910, while the second is an annotated bibliography of 369 research studies on classroom comprehension instruction. Of particular interest to reading researchers is the discussion by Faraone on three primary philosophical views of comprehension prominent during the earlier time period.

THORNDIKE, E.L. (1917). Reading as reasoning: A study of mistakes in paragraph reading. *Journal of Educational Psychology, 8*, 323–332.

>This is one of the most influential articles in reading education. Thorndike addresses the basic issue of what the reading process

entails, and he concludes that the process is as complex as thinking and is in fact a basic form of cognition. This article was destined to have far-reaching effects both for its time as well as today. (See the work of Edmund Huey on page 9 for a parallel study.)

THORNDIKE, E.L. (1921). *The teacher's wordbook.* New York: Bureau of Publications, Teachers College, Columbia University.

This publication was one of the first lists of vocabulary, based on the frequency of occurrence of these words taken from a variety of texts, for example, newspapers, trade books, and children's literature. Subsequent volumes included a teacher's book of 20,000 words and a teacher's word book of 30,000 words. This book had a major influence on the vocabulary selection of children's readers.

THORNDIKE, E.L. (1944). *The teacher's wordbook.* New York: Teachers College, Columbia University.

This book contains a list of 10,000 words with their range and frequency of occurrence, based on a sampling of various types of texts used commonly in schools. (An update of this book is Thorndike, E.L., & Lorge, I. [1944]. *The teacher's word book of 30,000 words.* New York: Bureau of Publications, Teachers College, Columbia University.)

SECTION SIX

Readability and Legibility of Text

A sentence should be read as if its author, had he held a plow instead of a pen, could have drawn a furrow deep and straight to the end.

Henry David Thoreau
A Week On the Concord and Merrimack, 1849

Determining the readability level of text has long been a concern of reading educators. Historically, the most prominent approach to this problem has been the use of various types of readability formulas. References in this section trace the development of these readability references and their various uses. In addition, in this section we have also included studies related to the legibility of text as well as the use of the cloze procedure.

GRAY, W.S. (1937). Progress in the study of readability. *Library Trends*, 237–254. Chicago: University of Chicago Press.

Gray reviews the important studies done in readability through 1937 in three areas: the origin of the readability movement, research completed in this area, and a study of the text elements that can frequently cause difficulty in reading.

KLARE, G.R. (1963). *The measurement of readability*. Ames, IA: Iowa State University Press.

This is the classic text in the historical study of readability measurement of print. This reference includes an extended discussion of the development and methodology of readability formulas with particular attention to the mathematical basis for many of these formulas. Of particular note is the bibliography that includes 482 annotated references.

LIVELY, B.A., & PRESSEY, S.L. (1923). A method for measuring the "vocabulary burden" of textbooks. *Educational Administration and Supervision, 9,* 389–398.

This article is considered to be one of the first references to the measurement of the readability of text through the use of a specific formula or method (see the Klare [1963] reference earlier in this section).

LORGE, I. (1944). Word lists as background for communication. *Teachers College Record, 51,* 543–552.

In this historical account of word lists as a foundation for readability, the author discusses the theoretical basis for these word counts as in the Teacher's Word Book (see Thorndike [1921, 1944] in Section Five, "Vocabulary and Comprehension").

McKENNA, M.C., & ROBINSON, R.D. (1980). *An introduction to the cloze procedure.* Newark, DE: International Reading Association.

This annotated bibliography is divided into nine areas related to the use of the cloze procedure, including readability measures. This is a good beginning reference for those interested in further study on the topic.

PATTERSON, D.G., & TINKER, M. (1940). *How to make type readable.* New York: Harper.

This review of the relation between typographic features and the understanding of printed text identifies 10 primary factors that can affect readers' understanding.

RANKIN, E.F. (1974). The cloze procedure revisited. In P.L. Nacke (Ed.), *Interaction: Research and Practice in College-Adult Reading*

(Twenty-third Yearbook of the National Reading Conference, pp. 1–8). Clemson, SC: National Reading Conference.

> This article is an overview of the cloze procedure, noting its use in various types of research including readability measurement.

TAYLOR, W.L. (1953). Cloze procedure: A new tool for measuring readability. *Journalism Quarterly, 30,* 415–433.

> This article introduces the term *cloze procedure*, defines it, and suggests various applications including its use as a readability measure.

TINKER, M. (1966). The ten most important legibility studies—An annotated bibliography. *The Reading Teacher, 20,* 46–58.

> The author identifies what he considers significant studies done in the field of legibility. This is an important reference for those wishing to conduct further work in this area.

SECTION SEVEN
Readiness

The impact of even one good book on a child's mind is surely an end in itself, a valid experience which helps him form standards of judgment and taste at the time when his mind is most sensitive to impressions of every kind.

Lillian H. Smith
The Unreluctant Years, 1953

The point at which a child is "ready to read" has long been a contentious one among reading educators. Opinions on this issue have ranged along a continuum from those who believed there were specific, measurable characteristics that would determine a child's eventual success or failure in reading to others who held to the viewpoint that readiness is a continuous process rather than a specific point in time. Included in this section are references reflecting the wide historical disparity in views on the topic of readiness.

DOMAN, G. (1963). *How to teach your baby to read: The gentle revolution.* New York: Random House.

>	This book represents an extreme position in advocating the teaching of reading to very young children, some as early as 10 months of age. Although most educators felt this position related to readiness was untenable, the general public readily accepted many of these ideas about early reading.

DURKIN, D. (1966). *Children who read early*. New York: Teachers College Press.

> This study reports on the characteristics of children who begin to read before formal education has begun. It emphasizes the importance of the home, especially the role of parents in helping their children develop as readers.

DURKIN, D. (1968). When should children begin to read? In H.M. Robinson (Ed.), *Innovation and change in reading instruction* (Sixty-seventh Yearbook of the National Society for the Study of Education, Part II, pp. 30–71). Chicago: University of Chicago Press.

> This paper is an excellent review of the history of readiness research. The studies are divided according to instructional concerns as they relate to readiness and secondly, how these procedures affect individual students.

GATES, A.I. (1937). The necessary mental age for beginning reading. *The Elementary School Journal, 37,* 497–508.

> Refutes the results of the Morphett and Washburn study (see later in this section), concluding that a specific mental age for beginning reading is a misleading indicator of eventual reading success.

GATES, A.I., BOND, G.L., & RUSSELL, D.H. (1939). *Methods of determining readiness*. New York: Bureau of Publications, Teachers College, Columbia University.

> This monograph, written by three historical leaders in reading education, is an important reference in the measurement of reading readiness, particularly in reference to the effectiveness of these various types of assessments. Of note is the caution these authors express concerning the negative predictability of many of the then existent reading readiness tests.

MASON, J.M. (1984). Early reading from a developmental perspective. In P.D. Pearson, R. Barr, M.L. Kamil, & P. Mosenthal (Eds.), *Handbook of reading research* (pp. 505–543). New York: Longman.

This chapter discusses the changes in thinking about reading readiness, now called "emergent reading," and how this change in thinking affected teachers and classroom behaviors. No longer was it believed there were specific characteristics necessary for beginning reading, but rather, this process was an ongoing one from birth throughout a lifetime.

MORPHETT, M.V., & WASHBURN, C. (1931). When should children learn to read? *The Elementary School Journal, 31*, 496–503.

An important historical article that had a major effect on the early teaching of reading. The results suggested that children should not receive formal training in reading until they had achieved a mental age of 6 years, 6 months. Despite the fact that the results of this research were quickly disputed by the reading community, many educators based teaching practices on these results for many years.

SULZBY, E., & TEAL, W. (1991). Emergent literacy. In R. Barr, M.L. Kamil, P. Mosenthal, & P.D. Pearson (Eds.), *Handbook of reading research: Volume II* (pp. 727–757). White Plains, NY: Longman.

This continuation of the discussion of emergent reading (see Mason [1984] in this section) concentrates on the review of research studies concerning the nature and attributes of young children's reading development. Of particular interest to reading researchers is the excellent bibliography of related resources.

SECTION EIGHT
Reading Disabilities and Remediation

I have had some [students] who have been with me, two, or three years, before they could read well. And that which hath yet been much more grievous to me. I have been so abashed and ashamed, that I have not known what to say, when some being a little discontented, or taking occasion to quarrel about paying my stipend, have cast this in my teeth, that their children have been under me six or seven years, and have yet not learned to read English well.

F. Kyngston
The Grammar School, 1627

From almost the beginning of reading instruction there have been students who experienced a wide variety of problems learning to read. The references in this section provide a good overview of the history of the diagnosis and remediation of reading disabilities. Of particular note in the study of language problems is the book, *Bibliography on the Problems Related to the Analysis, Prevention, and Correction of Reading Difficulties* (Betts, 1934), which is discussed in this monograph in Section Two, "Summaries of Reading Research."

BARRY, A.L. (1994). The staffing of high school remedial reading programs in the United States since 1920. *Journal of Reading, 38,* 14–22.

This article discusses the role of the remedial reading teacher in the high school setting with particular emphasis on the role of content teachers in the teaching of reading within their disciplines. Notes that in many schools the English or language arts teacher is considered the reading teacher.

BETTS, E.A. (1936). *The prevention and correction of reading difficulties*. Evanston: IL: Row, Peterson.

This is an important book on the assessment and remediation of reading problems. Of particular importance to researchers is the extensive discussion of the role of eye movements in reading as well as hand/eye preferences. This work also includes an early discussion of the role of the reading clinic, its organization, and functions. This volume is particularly important for the number of related references that are included.

DOLCH, E.W. (1939). *A manual of remedial reading*. Champaign, IL: Garrard Press.

This is an important early book in the field of assessment and remediation of reading disabilities. Of particular note is the emphasis on the role of the classroom teacher in the prevention and correction of reading problems. It includes an interesting discussion of the use of the ophthalmograph for eye movement photography and the metronoscope for tachistoscopic training.

FERNALD, G.M. (1943). *Remedial techniques in basic school subjects*. New York: McGraw-Hill.

This book deals primarily with remedial techniques the author considered important in language development, especially reading. This reference is an excellent overview of how the author believed students with reading difficulties could be helped. She advocates a multikinaesthetic approach to literacy acquisition.

FERNALD, G., & KELLER, H. (1921). The effect of kinaesthetic factors in the development of word recognition in the case of non-readers. *Journal of Educational Research, 4,* 355–377.

This is one of the early studies on the debated issue of the effect of kinaesthetic factors on reading disability. Fernald became a leader in this movement, which was to have a major influence on the teaching of reading for many years.

GATES, A.I. (1927). *The improvement of reading.* New York: Macmillan.

The role of the classroom teacher as being a principal aspect of the diagnosis and remediation of reading problems is the foundation of this textbook. Specific information is given as to how teachers can use a variety of assessment and remedial practices in the classroom setting. This textbook is a pioneering discussion of the importance of the teacher in these remediation activities, and is frequently referenced by others in subsequent reading publications.

HARRIS, A.J. (1940). *How to increase reading ability: A guide to diagnostic and remedial methods.* New York: Longman, Green and Co.

This textbook is a classic in the field of reading diagnosis and remediation, and is noted for its completeness in its discussion of the causes of reading problems and its extensive suggestions for assessment and correction of these difficulties. Written during the early development of reading clinics, this book often was used in the training of clinicians and as a resource in these facilities. This text has been reissued numerous times through a ninth edition (1990).

MONROE, M. (1932). *Children who cannot read.* Chicago: University of Chicago Press.

This is an early study of the quantitative and qualitative measurement of reading disability. Of particular interest is the detailed reporting of the results of various assessment procedures of the time and the insightful discussion of these results, especially in relation to various educational and social influences on a child's reading development.

ORTON, S.T. (1925). Word-blindness in school children. *Archives of neurology and psychiatry, 24,* 581–615.

> This article is one of the earliest reported studies investigating the relation between neurological disorders and reading disabilities. Terms such as *strephosymbolia* and *cortical elaboration* also were used to describe these reading problems.

ROBINSON, H.M. (1946). *Why pupils fail in reading: A study of causes and remedial treatment.* Chicago: University of Chicago Press.

> This is considered a landmark work in the history of the diagnosis and remediation of reading difficulties. It is one of the first studies to treat reading disability as being the result of multiple causation. The diagnosis of 30 students with severe reading disabilities was done by a team of medical and educational specialists using a case-study format. Remediation techniques for these students were based on the collective findings of a review panel.

SECTION NINE
Reading Assessment

Reading is to translate, for not two persons' experiences are the same.

W.H. Auden
The Dyer's Hand: Reading, 1962

From the earliest period in reading education, the effective measurement of reading ability has been an issue of concern. Early work on the study of eye movements (see Anderson & Dearborn, 1952, in Section Three, "Reading Paradigms, Perception, and Word Recognition") set the stage for the study or measurement of reading as a cognitive process. The references in this section have been selected to give the reading researcher a foundation or beginning in the study of the measurement of reading skills.

BROWN, J., GOODMAN, K.S., & MAREK, A.M. (1996). *Studies in miscue analysis: An annotated bibliography.* Newark, DE: International Reading Association.

> This book details the historical background of miscue analysis, beginning with studies as early as 1898. Of particular interest to history of reading researchers is the chronological order in which these miscue studies are arranged.

BUSWELL, G.T. (1920). *An experimental study of the eye-voice span in reading.* Chicago: University of Chicago Press.

This study was one of the first to begin the "formal" assessment of reading skills through the use of experimental design. It established a research model that was to be used by many others in the study or measurement of reading skills.

CALFEE, R., & HIEBERT, E. (1991). Classroom assessment of reading. In R. Barr, M.L. Kamil, P. Mosenthal, & P.D. Pearson (Eds.), *Handbook of reading research: Volume II* (pp. 281–309). White Plains, NY: Longman.

This review of reading assessment details the early development of the measurement of reading with particular emphasis on the use of various types of tests in the classroom setting. Of particular note for the reading researcher is the extensive bibliography that is included in this article. (See Johnston, 1984, in this section for reference to the first volume.)

GRAY, W.S. (1915/1916). Methods of testing reading, I. Methods of testing reading, II. *The Elementary School Journal, 1*, 231–246; 281–298.

This early article by Gray describes the beginnings of reading assessment with particular emphasis on the development of various types of diagnostic procedures.

JOHNSTON, P.H. (1984). Assessment in reading. In P.D. Pearson, R. Barr, M.L. Kamil, & P. Mosenthal (Eds.), *Handbook of reading research* (pp. 147–182). New York: Longman.

This work describes the development and the use of various types of reading assessment procedures then in use. For the reading researcher, this reference is of interest in its extensive discussion of the development, construction, and various related issues associated with the use of standardized tests as measures of reading development (see Calfee & Hiebert, 1991, earlier in this section).

VENEZKY, R.L. (1984). The history of reading research. In P.D. Pearson, R. Barr, M.L. Kamil, & P. Mosenthal (Eds.), *Handbook of reading research* (pp. 3–38). New York: Longman.

Although this entire volume is reviewed elsewhere (see Section Two, "Summaries of Reading Research"), this particular article is of importance in describing the early history of reading assessment. Following are some early reading tests:

Burgess, M.A. (1921). *A scale for measuring ability in silent reading.* New York: Russell Sage Foundation.

Dearborn, W.F., & Westbrook, C.H. (1921). *A silent reading test.* Cambridge, MA: Dearborn & Westbrook

Dolch, E.W. (1926). *Basic sight vocabulary cards test.* Champaign, IL: Garrard Press.

Durrell, D. (1932). *Durrell analysis of reading difficulty.* Yonkers-on-Hudson, NY: World Book.

Gates, A.I. (1931). *Gates reading survey test.* New York: Bureau of Publications, Teachers College, Columbia University.

Gray, W.S. (1915). *Standardized oral reading tests.* Bloomington, IN: Public School Publishers.

Haggerty, M.E., & Eurich, A.C. (1929). *A test of reading comprehension.* Minneapolis, MN: University of Minnesota.

SECTION TEN
Texts for Reading Instruction

'Tis a good reader that makes a good book.

> Ralph Waldo Emerson
> *Society and Solitude: Success*, 1870

The resources listed in this section deal with the various types of instructional materials that have been used for reading instruction. These include positive and negative references to the basal reader as well as historical discussions of past children's instructional materials. Venezky's (1990) and Michael's (1987, 1993) books provide excellent resources on U.S. and British primary resources in this area as well.

FLESCH, R. (1955). *Why Johnny can't read*. New York: Harper & Row.
In this work, Flesch attacks not only the prevailing whole word ("look and say") method of reading instruction and the basal readers that embodied it but the reading educators who authored them. The author advocates a synthetic phonics approach to reading instruction. This book received wide publicity by the U.S. media and thus had an important impact on society's attitudes concerning the effective teaching of phonics. The book was criticized by many educators as being an overly simplified answer to a very complex reading problem.

HOFFMAN, J.V., & ROSER, N. (Eds.). (1987). The basal reader in American reading instruction. *The Elementary School Journal, 87*, 243–384.

> The use of the basal reader for reading instruction has been historically a relatively common instructional practice. This volume addresses a number of issues related directly to the use of the basal reader including the evaluation and selection of these materials, forms of discourse in basal readers, and rethinking the role of these instructional materials in the typical classroom setting.

LUKE, A. (1988). *Literacy textbooks and ideology: Postwar literacy and the mythology of Dick and Jane.* London: Falmer Press.

> This book presents a Canadian reading perspective for the years 1946 to 1960. This scholarly presentation details the social pressures that shaped the development of reading instruction, particularly as this relates to teaching philosophy and various classroom techniques used in the teaching of reading skills.

MICHAEL, I. (1987). *The teaching of English from the sixteenth century to 1870.* London: Cambridge University Press.

> This book is considered by many to be the standard reference work on the historical development of English as a curriculum subject. Subjects such as oral and written expression, literature, and linguistic skills are covered in detail. Special emphasis is given to the methods instructors of the past used in teaching these subjects. Of particular note for reading researchers is the historical bibliography of more than 1,700 references, making this book one of the most important resources in any study of the pedagogical history of language instruction.

MICHAEL, I. (1993). *Early textbooks of English: A guide.* Reading, UK: University of Reading, Reading and Language Information Centre.

> This short monograph is an important reference for those interested in studying the early history of reading education in Great

Britain. References included in this scholarly volume are from the period 1530 through 1870 and represent most of the important titles in the field of reading from this period. The extensive annotations give details for each volume, not only as to author and publication but also the influence of the particular book on the history of reading. Also of great value is a discussion and bibliography of modern works on the study of the history of reading. This is a foundational reference for researchers who are interested in the roots of reading.

MONAGHAN, E.J. (1983). *A common heritage: Noah Webster's blue-back speller*. Hamden, CT: Archon Books.

Historical discussion of this important school textbook, which has been described with the New England Primer as being two of the most influential books in U.S. educational history. This speller was the work that taught children to read in the early American Republic as the embodiment of the old alphabet method of teaching reading. In its various editions, Webster's speller eventually sold at least 70 million copies.

RUSSELL, D.H. (1949). *Children learn to read*. Boston: Ginn.

This book features an important description of the teaching of reading following World War II with special emphasis on the use of basal readers and the whole word approach to reading instruction.

SHANNON, P. (1989). *Broken promises: Reading instruction in twentieth-century America*. New York: Bergin & Garvey.

Shannon makes the case that, historically, U.S. reading instruction has not treated all students fairly. He notes, for example, that groups such as women, minorities, and the poor often have been excluded from formal reading instruction in various ways. This book contains an excellent bibliography of related materials with an emphasis on the politics of reading and the language arts.

SMITH, N.B. (1934). *American reading instruction*. New York: Silver Burdett. (Reprinted in 1965 by the International Reading Association, Newark, DE.)

> This book is considered to be a classic in the field. Although others have added to Smith's original work, this study is a foundational reference for anyone wishing to study the historical field of reading instruction. Most of the author's analysis is based on a review of many primary reading materials. (See the reference to Smith, 1986, in this section for an updated edition of this book).

SMITH, N.B. (1986). *American reading instruction*. Newark, DE: International Reading Association. (Original work published 1934) (This 1986 edition contains a prologue by Leonard Courtney and epilogue by H. Alan Robinson.)

> This updated edition of *American Reading Instruction* adds 21 years of new reading research and practice to the original volume. For those who want a general overview of the history of U.S. reading instruction, this reference is an excellent beginning point. (See the reference to Venezky, 1990, in this section for further information on reading materials.)

SPIKER, T.M. (1997). *Dick and Jane go to church: A history of the Cathedral Readers*. Unpublished doctoral dissertation, University of Pittsburgh, Pittsburgh, PA.

> The Cathedral Readers were a version of the Dick and Jane readers published for the Catholic schools of North America. This research on these readers is a comprehensive review of the reasons for the development of the Cathedral Readers, how they differed from those materials used in the public schools, and basic changes in these materials from their inception in the 1920s through the late 1960s. Of particular note to reading historians is a bibliography of more than 40 pages.

VENEZKY, R.L. (1990). *American primers*. Bethesda, MD: University Publications of America.

This is perhaps the most complete collection of information available on existing historical readers of various types. It includes a bibliography of 844 sources, available on microfilm, which should prove invaluable for the reading researcher.

SECTION ELEVEN

Professional References
Related to the Teaching of Reading

It is more profitable to reread old books than to read new ones,
just as it is better to repair and add to an old temple than to build
one entirely new.

Chang Chao
Yumengying, before 1693

The following list of books has been compiled primarily for
those researchers interested in the pedagogy of reading, especially from an historical perspective. Although these references
are listed without annotation, the titles in most cases indicate
contents of specific volumes. Almost all the books contain extensive descriptions of classroom procedures associated with
reading instruction, as well as descriptions of related materials.

ADAMS, F., GRAY, L., & REESE, D. (1949). *Teaching children to read.*
New York: Ronald Press.

ANDERSON, C.J., & DAVIDSON, I. (1925). *Reading objectives: A guide-
book on the teaching of reading.* New York: Laurel Books.

BETTS, E.A. (1946). *Foundations of reading instruction.* New York:
American Book.

BOND, G.L., & BOND, E. (1943). *Teaching the child to read.* New York: Macmillan.

BRIGGS, T.H., & COFFMAN, L.D. (1908). *Reading in the public schools.* Chicago: Row Peterson.

BROOKS, E. (1879). *Normal methods of teaching.* Lancaster, PA: Normal Publishing Company. (Contains important section on the teaching of reading).

BROOKS, E. (1885). *Elocution and reading.* Philadelphia: Eldredge & Brother.

BROOM, M.E., DUNCAN, M.A., EMIG, D., & STUBER, J. (1942). *Effective reading instruction in the elementary school.* New York: McGraw-Hill.

BRUECKNER, L.J., & MELBY, E.O. (1931). *Diagnostic and remedial teaching.* Boston: Houghton Mifflin.

CARTER, H.L., & McGINNIS, D.J. (1953). *Learning to read: A handbook for teachers.* New York: McGraw-Hill.

CLARK, S.H. (1898). *How to teach reading in the public schools.* Chicago: Scott, Foresman.

DOLCH, E.W. (1950). *Teaching primary reading.* Champaign, IL: Garrard Press.

DURRELL, D.D. (1940). *Improvement of basic reading abilities.* Yonkers-on-Hudson, New York: World Books.

HAMILL, S.S. (1891). *New science of elocution.* New York: Hunt & Eaton.

HARRISON, M.L. (1936). *Reading readiness.* Boston: Houghton Mifflin.

HERBER, H.L. (1970). *Teaching reading in content areas.* Englewood Cliffs, NJ: Prentice Hall.

KIRK, S.A., & MONROE, M. (1940). *Teaching reading to slow-learning children.* Boston: Houghton Mifflin.

KLAPPER, P. (1914). *Teaching children to read.* New York: D. Appleton.

KNIGHT, P.E., & TRAXLER, A.E. (1937). *Read and comprehend.* Boston: Little, Brown.

KOTTMEYER, W. (1947). *Handbook for remedial reading.* St. Louis, MO: Webster Publishing.

LEONARD, J.P., & SALISBURY, R. (1941). *Considering the meaning.* Chicago: Scott, Foresman.

MCCALLISTER, J.M. (1936). *Remedial and corrective instruction in reading.* New York: D. Appleton-Century.

MCKEE, P. (1934). *Reading and literature in the elementary school.* Boston: Houghton Mifflin.

MCKEE, P. (1939). *Language in the elementary school.* Boston: Houghton Mifflin.

MCKEE, P. (1948). *The teaching of reading in the elementary school.* Boston: Houghton Mifflin.

MONROE, M. (1951). *Growing into reading.* Chicago: Scott, Foresman.

Monroe, M., & Backus, B. (1937). *Remedial reading.* Boston: Houghton Mifflin.

Norvell, G.W. (1950). *The reading interests of young people.* Boston: D.C. Heath.

O'Brien, J.A. (1926). *Reading: Its psychology and pedagogy.* New York: The Century Company.

Patterson, S.W. (1930). *Teaching a child to read.* Garden City, New York: Doubleday, Doran & Co.

Pennell, M.E., & Cusak, A.M. (1924). *How to teach reading.* Boston: Houghton Mifflin.

Schonell, F.J. (1945). *The psychology and teaching of reading.* London: Oliver & Boyd.

Sherman, E.B., & Reed, A.A. (1909). *Essentials of teaching reading.* Chicago: The University Publishing Company.

Stone, C.R. (1922). *Silent and oral reading.* Boston: Houghton Mifflin. (Good examples of bibliography listings on pages 297–298).

Storm, G.E., & Smith, N.B. (1930). *Reading activities in the primary grades.* Boston: Ginn.

Strang, R., & Rose, F.C. (1938). *Problems in the improvement of reading in high school and college.* Lancaster, PA: Science Press Printing.

Tenney, E.A., & Wardle, R.M. (1942). *A primer for readers.* New York: Appleton-Century-Crofts.

TINKER, M. (1952). *Teaching elementary reading.* New York: Appleton-Century-Crofts.

TURNER, N.E. (1915). *Teaching to read.* New York: American Book Company.

UHL, W.L. (1924). *The materials of reading.* New York: Silver Burdett

WHEAT, H.G. (1923). *The teaching of reading.* New York: Ginn.

WHITE, E.E. (1886). *The elements of pedagogy.* New York: American Book.

WITTY, P. (1949). *Reading in modern education.* Boston: D.C. Heath.

WITTY, P. (1953). *How to become a better reader.* Chicago: Science Research Associates.

WITTY, P., & KOPPEL, D. (1939). *Reading and the educative process.* New York: Ginn.

YOAKAM, G.A. (1928). *Reading and study.* New York: Macmillan.

ZIRBES, L. (1925). *Practice exercises and checks on silent reading in the primary grades.* New York: Columbia University, The Lincoln School of the Teachers College.

SECTION TWELVE
Reading Educators

Give a man this taste [for reading] and you [the teacher] can hardly fail to make him a happy man. You place him in contact with the best society in every period of history, with the wisest and wittiest, the tenderest and bravest who have adorned humanity.

John Herschel
at the opening of Eton Library, 1833

The field of reading education has had a significant number of influential educators who have made major contributions, both in reading as well as other related educational fields. In this section are listed references dealing with former leaders in the field of reading education.

KLINE, E., MOORE, D.W., & MOORE, S. (1987). Colonial Francis Parker and beginning reading instruction. *Reading Research and Instruction, 26,* 141–150.

> An important contribution to the historical study of early educators and their thinking and influence on the teaching of reading. This article describes Parker's approach to reading instruction that was based to a large degree on the importance of connections between what the reader was reading and the individual's past background and interests, current educational purposes, and the material being read. Many of Parker's ideas reflect modern thinking associated with current reading instruction.

MAVROGENES, N.A. (1985). *William Scott Gray: Leader of teachers and shaper of American reading instruction.* Unpublished doctoral dissertation, University of Chicago, Chicago, Illinois.

William S. Gray's influence on reading education is evident in this volume, not only in what he published but also his influence on other contemporary reading researchers as well as his work's continuing importance for today's reading efforts. Other references include the following:

MAVROGENES, N.A. (1985). *William S. Gray and the Dick and Jane readers.* (ERIC Document Reproduction Service No. ED 269 722).

This reference details the influence and work of Gray in the development of one of the most influential basal reading series in the United States.

MAVROGENES, N.A. (1985). William S. Gray: The person. In J. Stevenson (Ed.), *William S. Gray: Teacher, scholar, leader* (1–23). Newark, DE: International Reading Association.

A discussion of the personal life of Gray noting his educational background as well as his professional teaching and research history.

MOORE, D. (1986). Laura Zirbes and progressive reading instruction. *The Elementary School Journal, 86,* 663–672.

This historical study of Laura Zirbes, a pioneer in the field of reading education, describes her influence on both reading practices in the classroom setting of her day as well as her important early reading research. This important article, one of the few on early reading figures, should serve as a model for other researchers to follow.

STEVENSON, J.A. (ED.). (1985). *William S. Gray, teacher, scholar, leader.* Newark, DE: International Reading Association.

GUTHRIE, J.T. (1984). *Reading, William S. Gray: A research retrospective, 1881–1941.* Newark, DE: International Reading Association.

These two books complement each other in their descriptions of William S. Gray, considered by many to be one of the leading scholars in the field of reading education. Stevenson's book places Gray in the context of his work as a university professor, with particular emphasis on his influence at all educational levels related to the teaching of reading. Guthrie's work details the extensive and very influential research of Gray in many areas of reading. Together these two books provide an excellent discussion of the lifetime work of Gray.

In studying the life of William S. Gray, it should be noted that Mavrogenes's bibliography in Stevenson (1985) covers Gray's life to 1916. Of particular interest to reading historians in this book is a complete bibliography of Gray's published works.

SULLIVAN, D.P. (1994). *William Holmes McGuffey: Schoolmaster to the nation.* Rutherford, NJ: Fairleigh Dickinson University Press.

> William McGuffey's influence on the teaching practices and reading interests of early U.S. education was profound. Almost every child and teacher was influenced by the extended use of the McGuffey Readers at all levels from primer through the higher grade levels. This is an important volume for those interested in the history of an individual who shaped reading policy and classroom practices.

VANCE, E. (1985). *Classroom reading and the work of Arthur Gates: 1921–1930.* Unpublished doctoral dissertation, Columbia University, New York.

> Arthur Gates was an important early reading educator who developed a definition of reading built on theoretical presuppositions and then shaped by classroom practices and conditions. This thesis examines Gates's significant contribution to reading education, particularly as it relates to the teacher's role in effective reading instruction.

The *History of Reading News*, the official publication of the History of Reading Special Interest Group of the International Reading Association, has at various times published articles on leaders in the field. These materials are either personal reminiscences by a particular person about his or her life as reading educator, or are memoirs written by colleagues. The following is a selected list of these references:

Nila Banton Smith (M)	Vol. II, No. 1 (April, 1977), 1–2.
William S. Gray (M)	Vol. IX, No. 1 (Fall, 1985), 1.
Helen M. Robinson (M)	Vol. XII, No. 1 (Fall, 1988), 1.
Ralph Staiger (Part 1) (A)	Vol. XII, No. 1 (Fall, 1988), 1.
(Part 2) (A)	Vol. XIII, No. 1 (Fall, 1989), 2–3.
Theodore Clymer (A)	Vol. XIV, No. 1 (Fall, 1990), 1.
Albert Harris (M)	Vol. XV, No. 1 (Fall, 1991), 6.
Walter MacGinitie (A)	Vol. XV, No. 1 (Fall, 1991), 2, 7.
Olive S. Niles (M)	Vol. XVI, No. 1 (Fall, 1992), 1–2.
Jeanne S. Chall (Part 1) (A)	Vol. XVII, No. 1 (Fall, 1993), 1–2.
(Part 2) (A)	Vol. XVII, No. 2 (Spring, 1994), 2.
A. Garr Cranney (M)	Vol. XIX, No. 1 (Fall, 1995), 1–8.
Nancy Larrick (A)	Vol. XIX, No. 2 (Spring, 1996), 1–3.
H. Alan Robinson (A)	Vol. XXI, No. 1 (Fall, 1997), 1–2; 6–7.
John Elkins (A)	Vol. XX1, No. 2 (Spring, 1998), 1–2.
Grace Fernald (M)	Vol. XX1, No. 2 (Spring, 1998), 6–8.
Sidney J. Rauch (A)	Vol. XXII, No. 1 (Fall, 1998), 1–2, 78.
A. Sterl Artley (M)	Vol. XXII, No. 1 (Fall, 1998), 6.

(A) Autobiographical material written by the subject.

(M) Memoir, written by someone else.

These references to reading educators are listed in the Author Index by their last names, in the Title Index under the general terms "Autobiographical Material" or "Memoirs," and in the Subject Index under "Reading Educators."

SECTION THIRTEEN
Writing

> The greatest part of a writer's time is spent in reading, in order to write; a man will turn over half a library to make one book.
>
> Samuel Johnson
> *Boswell's Life*, 1775

The study of writing is an important aspect of the total language arts program. Although there is no attempt to include all the many possible sources related to writing in this section, the following volumes have been selected for these reasons: importance in terms of their effect on classroom instruction in writing, theoretical positions presented by the various authors, and having the most influence historically on the field of reading education. This is a very limited selection of what could be included in relation to the total field of writing and reading.

BISSEX, G. (1980). *GYNS AT WK: A child learns to write and read.* Cambridge, MA: Harvard University Press.

> This important book details the growth of the author's son as both a reader and writer. It is a particularly important reference in terms of detailing purposes for writing. It reflects much of the current theory and practice in the teaching of writing.

BRITTON, B. (1970). *Language and learning.* Middlesex, UK: Penguin Books.

Britton's work was destined to provide an important theoretical foundation for much of the work being done today in the area of writing. This volume is perhaps his most inclusive statement regarding the influences of experience and society on the process and product of a writer.

CALKINS, L.M. (1981). *Lessons from a child: On the teaching and learning of writing.* Portsmouth, NH: Heinemann.

In much the same format as Bissex (see the reference earlier in this section), Calkins uses one child (Susie) as a model for the effective teaching of writing. Although the text centers on the progress made in writing by Susie, the information in this book is reflective of the writing activities of a much larger group of approximately 150 students. For those interested in the historical development of writing, this is an important reference.

COULMAS, F. (1989). *The writing systems of the world.* Oxford, UK: Basil Blackwell.

This book is an excellent example of an entire genre of books related to the history of writing in its many forms. Of particular interest to reading researchers is the extensive bibliography.

ELBOW, P. (1981). *Writing with power: Techniques for mastering the writing process.* New York: Oxford University Press.

This is an important contribution to the field of writing, especially as it relates to the teaching of this subject in the classroom setting. This book is an early discussion of how students can be taught to write more effectively.

EMIG, J. (1971). *The composing processes of twelfth graders.* Urbana, IL: National Council of Teachers of English.

Through the use of a case-study approach, Emig examined the composing processes of eight twelfth graders as they created autobiographies of their writing experiences. The conclusions of this seminal work had major implications for changes in the instructional procedures used by teachers of writing.

GRAVES, D. (1983). *Writing: Teachers and children at work.* Portsmouth, NH: Heinemann.

> Donald Graves has had a major influence on many of the current themes and strategies used by classroom teachers today in their teaching of writing. This volume is a good overview of Graves's theory, and shows his ideas related to writing applied in a classroom setting.

MONAGHAN, E.J. (ED.). (1987). Then and now: Readers learning to write. *Visible Language, 21,* 161–302.

> The history of the teaching of writing has only recently begun to receive attention from historians. This volume contains five articles on various aspects of writing, such as the curriculum of the writing schools of the 18th century in Boston and writing as praxis during the period 1900 to 1959. This collection of articles spans the time period from the 18th century to emergent literacy in the 20th century.

MURPHY, J. (1990). *Short history of writing instruction from ancient Greece to twentieth-century America.* Davis, CA: Hermagoras Press.

> This important volume traces the history of writing from its earliest beginnings in ancient Greece and Rome. Important topics covered in this text include Roman writing as described by Quintilian, the teaching of writing in medieval Europe, and writing instruction in Great Britain in the 18th and 19th centuries.

SECTION FOURTEEN

Historical Dissertations in Reading Education

There is no Frigate like a book
To take us lands away
Not any Coursers like a Page
Of prancing Poetry

Emily Dickenson
Complete Poems, "No. 1263," 1873

Dissertation research in the area of reading education has had an important influence on classroom practices as well as fundamental investigations in this area. The following selected dissertations represent a very small sample of what could be included in this section. In helping to guide the development of this list, reference was made to the membership list of the International Reading Association's Reading Hall of Fame. An arbitrary date of 1955 also was used in the final selection of these dissertations. It is interesting to note how dissertation research tended to influence individuals and their work in reading education for much of their professional lives.

ALLEN, R.V. (1948). *The development and application of criteria for appraising reading programs in elementary schools.* Austin, TX: The University of Texas.

ARTLEY, A.S. (1942). *A study of certain relationships existing between general reading comprehension and reading comprehension in a specific subject-matter area.* Unpublished doctoral dissertation, Pennsylvania State University, State College.

BETTS, E. (1931). *An experimental appraisal of certain techniques for the study of oral composition.* Unpublished doctoral dissertation, University of Iowa, Iowa City.

BOND, E. (1939). *Reading and ninth grade achievement.* Unpublished doctoral dissertation, Columbia University, New York, NY.

BOND, G. (1936). *The auditory and speech characteristics of poor readers.* Unpublished doctoral dissertation, Columbia University, New York, NY.

BUSWELL, G. (1920). *An experimental study of the eye-voice span in reading.* Unpublished doctoral dissertation, the University of Chicago, Chicago, IL.

CLYMER, T. (1952). *The influence of reading ability on the validity of group intelligence tests.* Unpublished doctoral dissertation, the University of Minnesota, Minneapolis.

DAVIS, F.B. (1950). *Fundamental factors of comprehension in reading.* Harvard University, Cambridge, MA.

DEARBORN, W. (1905). *Psychology of reading.* Unpublished doctoral dissertation, Columbia University, New York, NY.

DOLCH, E.W. (1925). *Reading and word meanings.* Unpublished doctoral dissertation, University of Illinois, Urbana.

FAY, L. (1949). *The relationship between specific reading skills and selected areas of sixth-grade achievement.* Unpublished doctoral dissertation, University of Minnesota, Minneapolis.

GANS, R. (1940). *A study of critical reading comprehension in the intermediate grades.* Unpublished doctoral dissertation, Columbia University, New York, NY.

GATES, A. (1917). *Recitation as a factor in memorizing.* Unpublished doctoral dissertation, Columbia University, New York, NY.

GRAY, W.S. (1916). *Studies of elementary-school reading through standardized tests.* Unpublished doctoral dissertation, University of Chicago, Chicago, IL.

HARRIS, T. (1941). *A laboratory study of the relation of selected factors to the span of recognition in silent reading.* Unpublished doctoral dissertation, University of Chicago, Chicago, IL.

HOLMES, J.A. (1949). *Factors underlying major reading disabilities at the college level.* Unpublished doctoral dissertation, University of California, Berkeley.

HUEY, E. (1899). *On the psychology and physiology of reading.* Unpublished doctoral dissertation, Clark University, Worcester, MA.

HUUS, H. (1944). *Factors associated with the reading achievement of children from a migratory population.* Unpublished doctoral dissertation, University of Chicago, Chicago, IL.

McKEE, P. (1924). *Teaching spelling by column and context.* Unpublished doctoral dissertation, University of Iowa, Iowa City.

ROBINSON, H.M. (1945). *An investigation into the causes of severe reading retardation.* University of Chicago, Chicago, IL. This dissertation was published as a book titled *Why Pupils Fail in Reading* (see review of this book in Section One, "General Works In Reading").

SMITH, N.B. (1935). *A historical analysis of American reading instruction.* Columbia University, New York, NY. This dissertation was the foundation research for the book, *American Reading Instruction* (see the review of this book in Section One, "General Works in Reading").

TRAXLER, A.E. (1932). *The measurement and improvement of silent reading at the junior-high level.* Unpublished doctoral dissertation, University of Chicago, Chicago, IL.

UHL, W.L. (1921). *Scientific determination of the content of the elementary school course in reading.* Unpublished doctoral dissertation, University of Chicago, Chicago, IL.

WHIPPLE, G. (1936). *Procedures used in selecting textbooks.* Unpublished doctoral dissertation, University of Chicago, Chicago, IL.

YOAKAM, G. (1922). *The effect of a single reading on the retention of various types of material in the content subjects of the elementary school curriculum as measured by immediate and delayed recall.* Unpublished doctoral dissertation, University of Iowa, Iowa City.

ZIRBES, L. (1927). *Comparative studies of current practice in reading, with techniques for the improvement of teaching.* Unpublished doctoral dissertation, Columbia University, New York, NY.

SECTION FIFTEEN

Yearbooks and Organizations of Interest to Reading Educators

Books are the compasses and telescopes and sextents and charts which other men have prepared to help us navigate the dangerous seas of life.

Jesse Lee Beecher
Proverbs from Plymouth Pulpit, 1918.

This is a listing of some of the most significant yearbooks and organizations in the field of reading education. For researchers interested in the history of reading, these materials provide rich sources of information.

Yearbooks

CLAREMONT COLLEGE ANNUAL READING CONFERENCE. CLAREMONT, CA: Claremont College (annual meeting of the Claremont Graduate School of Education from 1936 to the present).

> This series of yearbooks was first published in 1936 and provides the reading historian with a useful collection of a variety of studies in reading education.

ANNUAL CONFERENCES ON READING HELD AT THE UNIVERSITY OF CHICAGO (annual meeting between the years 1939 and 1966).

The University of Chicago played a prominent role in the field of reading education. A significant part of this involvement was a series of reading conferences held between 1939 and 1966. In connection with these conferences, an annual yearbook was published under the editorship of the noted reading scholars William S. Gray, Helen Robinson, and H. Alan Robinson. These yearbooks are some of the most valuable resources in the historical study of reading education. Of particular note is the 1966 yearbook, published in connection with the 75th anniversary of the University of Chicago (*Reading: Seventy-Five Years of Progress* [Proceedings of the annual conference on reading held at the University of Chicago]. Chicago: University of Chicago). This particular edition is a summary of the work done in past years and is a particularly valuable reference.

NATIONAL SOCIETY FOR THE STUDY OF EDUCATION YEARBOOKS (various dates). Chicago: University of Chicago Press.

This series of landmark books deals with many critical issues in the field of reading education. Many of the chapters in the NSSE Yearbooks were written by leaders in the reading field and were often in the forefront of thinking on these issues. Of particular importance to the reading researcher are the extensive bibliographies included in many of these volumes. The following editions deal primarily with reading education: 20th (1921), 24th (1925), 36th (1937), 47th (1948), 48th (1949), 55th (1956), 60th (1961), 67th (1968), and 83rd (1984).

Reading Organizations

International Reading Association. The International Reading Association is the largest organization in the field of reading with an extensive publication history of both journals and books. Of particular interest to those working in the history of reading are the annual yearbooks based on annual conventions (the first yearbook was published in 1956 and was edited by William S. Gray; the last yearbook was published in 1970). For those studying various trends and issues in the field of reading, the publications of this organization are a valuable source of information.

History of Reading Special Interest Group of the International Reading Association. The purpose of this group, founded in 1975, is "to encourage historical research in the field of reading and literacy, to provide a forum for dissemination, and to promote the development of a body of historical knowledge about reading and literacy." This group publishes a semiannual newsletter titled the *History of Reading News*. This publication reviews the latest books on the study of reading history and keeps members apprised of new research and writing being done by members of the group. The newsletter also publishes reminiscences and memoirs of key figures in the field of reading education.

Typical of this Special Interest Group's publications is a recent booklet titled *Writing the Past: Teaching Reading in Colonial America and the United States 1640–1940* (Monaghan & Barry, 1999). This booklet was used to describe an exhibition of historical materials at the 44th Annual Convention of the International Reading Association in San Diego, California.

National Council of Teachers of English. This organization publishes a wide diversity of journals, books, and other publications on topics related to language arts. The early publications of this organization are an important resource for those working in the history of reading, writing, and literature.

National Reading Conference. The National Reading Conference, organized in 1952, has published a series of yearbooks that are of importance to reading research. These publications, many with extensive bibliographies such as the *Annual Reviews of Research*, are important reference points for scholars interested in the historical development of reading trends and issues.

Society for the History of Authorship, Reading, and Publishing (SHARP). The stated purpose of this organization is to provide a global network for book historians to meet, either electronically through e-mail or at an annual meeting, for the discussion of common themes and projects related to various issues involving the book. SHARP also has issued an annual periodical titled *Book History*.

Textbook Colloquium. The Textbook Colloquium, based in the United Kingdom, is an organization that has the stated purpose, "to study all aspects of the textbook." This group publishes a newsletter/journal titled *Paradigm* three times a year. Although not exclusively interested in reading, *Paradigm* frequently publishes material of interest to reading historians.

AUTHOR INDEX

Bissex, G. (1980). *GYNS AT WK: A child learns to write and read*, 61, 62

Bond, E. (1939). *Reading and ninth grade achievement*, 65

Bond, G. (1936). *The auditory and speech characteristics of poor readers*, 65

Bond, G.L., & Bond, E. (1943). *Teaching the child to read*, 53

Briggs, T.H., & Coffman, L.D. (1908). *Reading in the public schools*, 53

Britton, B. (1970). *Language and learning*, 61

Brooks, E. (1879). *Normal methods of teaching*, 53

Brooks, E. (1885). *Elocution and reading*, 53

Brooks, G., Pugh, A.K., & Hall, N. (1993). *Further studies in the history of reading*, 17

Broom, M.E., Duncan, M.A., Emig, D., & Stuber, J. (1942). *Effective reading instruction in the elementary school*, 53

Brown, J., Goodman, K.S., & Marek, A.M. (1996). *Studies in miscue analysis: An annotated bibliography*, 44

Brueckner, L.J., & Melby, E.O. (1931). *Diagnostic and remedial teaching*, 53

Burgess, M.A. (1921). *A scale for measuring ability in silent reading*, 46

Bury, R. de (1948). *The philobiblon* [The love of books], 8

Buswell, G.T. (1920). *An experimental study of the eye-voice span in reading*, 45, 65

Buswell, G.T. (1945). *Non-oral reading: A study of its use in the Chicago Public Schools*, 28

C

Calfee, R., & Hiebert, E. (1991). "Classroom assessment of reading," 45

Calkins, L.M. (1981). *Lessons from a child: On the teaching and learning of writing*, 62

Carter, H.L., & McGinnis, D.J. (1953). *Learning to read: A handbook for teachers*, 53

Chall, J.S. (1993, 1994). Autobiographical sketch in *History of Reading News*, 60

Chall, J.S. (1967). *Learning to read: The great debate*, 24

Clark, S.H. (1898). *How to teach reading in the public schools*, 53

Clifford, G.J. (1978). "Words for schools: The applications in education of the vocabulary of Edward L. Thorndike," 31

Clymer, T. (1952). *The influence of reading ability on the validity of group intelligence tests*, 65

Clymer, T. (1963). "The utility of phonics generalizations in the primary grades," 24

Clymer, T. (1990). Autobiographical sketch in the *History of Reading News*, 60

Cole, L. (1938). *The improvement of reading*, 24

Coulmas, F. (1989). *The writing systems of the world*, 62

Cranney, A.G., & Miller, J. (1987). "History of reading: Status and sources of a growing field," 9

Cranney, A.G. (1995). Memoir in the *History of Reading News*, 60

D

Davidson, C.N. (1989). *Reading in America: Literature and social history*, 9

Davis, F.B. (1950). *Fundamental factors of comprehension in reading*, 65

Dearborn, W. (1905). *Psychology of reading*, 65

Dearborn, W.F. (1906). (listed under Huey, 1908). *The psychology of reading: An experimental study of the reading process and eye movements*, 10

Dearborn, W.F., & Westbrook, C.H. (1921). *A silent reading test*, 46

Dodge, R. (1907). (listed under Huey, 1908). "An experimental study of visual fixation," 10

Dolch, E.W. (1925). *Reading and word meanings*, 65

Dolch, E.W. (1926). *Basic sight vocabulary cards test*, 46

Dolch, E.W. (1936). *A basic sight vocabulary*, 32

Dolch, E.W. (1939). *A manual for remedial reading*, 41

Dolch, E.W. (1950). *Teaching primary reading*, 53

Doman, G. (1963). *How to teach your baby to read: The gentle revolution*, 37

Downing, J.A. (1962). *The initial teaching alphabet*, 25

Downing, J.A. (1964). *The initial teaching alphabet reading experiment*, 25

Durkin, D. (1966). *Children who read early*, 38

Durkin, D. (1968). "When should children begin to read?," 38

Durrell, D. (1932). *Durrell analysis of reading difficulty*, 46

Durrell, D.D. (1940). *Improvement of basic reading abilities*, 53

E

Elbow, P. (1981). *Writing with power: Techniques for mastering the writing process*, 62

Elkins, J. (1998). Autobiographical sketch in the *History of Reading News*, 60

Emig, J. (1971). *The composing processes of twelfth graders*, 62

F

Fadiman, C. (1960). *The new lifetime reading plan* [listed under Adler (1940)], 8

Fay, L. (1949). *The relationship between specific reading skills and selected areas of sixth-grade achievement*, 66

Fernald, G.M. (1943). *Remedial techniques in basic school subjects*, 41

Fernald, G. (1998). Memoir in the *History of Reading News*, 60

Fernald, G., & Keller, H. (1921). "The effect of kinaesthetic factors in the development of word recognition in the case of non-readers," 41

Flesch, R. (1955). *Why Johnny can't read*, 47

G

Gans, R. (1940). *A study of critical reading comprehension in the intermediate grades*, 66

Gates, A. (1917). *Recitation as a factor in memorizing*, 66

Gates, A.I. (1927). *The improvement of reading*, 42

Gates, A.I. (1931). *Gates reading survey test*, 46

Gates, A.I. (1937). "The necessary mental age for beginning reading," 38

Gates, A.I., Bond, G.L., & Russell, D.H.

R

Rankin, E.F. (1974). "The cloze procedure revisited," 35

Rauch, S.J. (1998). Autobiographical sketch in the *History of Reading News*, 60

Rayner, K. (1997). "Understanding eye movements in reading," 23, 26

Robinson, H.A. (1997). Autobiographical sketch in the *History of Reading News*, 60

Robinson, H.A., Faraone, V., Hittleman, D.R., & Unruh, E. (1990). *Reading comprehension instruction 1783–1987: A review of trends and research*, 32

Robinson, H.M. (1945). *An investigation into the causes of severe reading retardation*, 66

Robinson, H.M. (1946). *Why pupils fail in reading: A study of causes and remedial treatment*, 43

Robinson, H.M. (1988). Memoir in the *History of Reading News*, 60

Robinson, R.D. (1989). "Reading teachers of the past—What they believed about reading," 3, 14

Robinson, R.D., Baker, E., & Clegg, L. (1998). Literacy and the pendulum of change: Lessons for the 21st century, 2, 3

Rohrer, J.H. (1943). "An analysis and evaluation of the non-oral method of reading instruction," 28, 29, 30

Russell, D.H. (1949). *Children learn to read*, 49

S

Saenger, P. (1997). *Space between words: The origins of silent reading*, 14, 30

Schonell, F. J. (1945). *The psychology and teaching of reading*, 55

Shannon, P. (1989). *Broken promises: Reading instruction in twentieth-century America*, 49

Sherman, E.B., & Reed, A.A. (1909). *Essentials of teaching reading*, 55

Smith, F. (1979). *Reading without nonsense* , 26

Smith, F. (1971). *Understanding reading: A psycholinguistic analysis of reading and learning to read*, 26

Smith, N.B. (1934, 1986). *American reading instruction*, 50

Smith, N.B. (1935). *A historical analysis of American reading instruction*, 67

Smith, N.B. (1966). "Reading: Seventy-five years of progress," 19

Smith, N.B. (1977). Memoir in the *History of Reading News*, 60

Spiker, T.M. (1997). *Dick and Jane go to church: A history of the Cathedral Readers*, 50

Stahl, N.A., & King, J.R. (2000). "A history of college reading," 19

Staiger, R. (1988, 1989). Autobiographical sketch in the *History of Reading News*, 60

Stevenson, J.A. (1985). *William S. Gray, Teacher, scholar, leader*, 58

Stone, C.R. (1922). *Silent and oral reading*, 55

Storm, G.E., & Smith, N.B. (1930). *Reading activities in the primary grades*, 55

Strang, R. (1939). *Bibliography relating to reading on the high school and college level*, 16, 20

Strang, R., & Rose, F.C. (1938). *Problems in the improvement of reading in high school and college*, 55

Sullivan, D.P. (1994). *William Holmes McGuffey: Schoolmaster to the nation*, 59

Education, Part II, 30

White, E.E. (1886). *The elements of pedagogy,* 56

Witty, P. (1953). *How to become a better reader,* 56

Witty, P. (1949). *Reading in modern education,* 56

Witty, P., & Koppel, D. (1939). *Reading and the educational process,* 56

Wood, E. (1963). "Speed reading," 15

Y

Yoakam, G. (1922). *The effect of a single reading on the retention of various types of material in the content subjects of the elementary school curriculum as measured by immediate and delayed recall,* 67

Yoakam, G.A. (1928). *Reading and study,* 56

Z

Zirbes, L. (1925). *Practice exercises and checks on silent reading in the primary grades,* 56

Zirbes, L. (1927). *Comparative studies of current practice in reading, with techniques for the improvement of teaching,* 67

TITLE INDEX

A

"The all white world of children's books." Larrick, N. (1965), 11

Alphabets and reading: The initial teaching alphabet. Pitman, J. (1969), 25

American primers. Venezky, R.L. (1990), 50

American reading instruction. Smith, N.B. (1934, 1986), 50, 61

"An analysis and evaluation of the non-oral method of reading instruction." Rohrer, J.H. (1943), 30

Ancient literacy. Harris, W.V. (1989), 9

"Ancient reading." Henrickson, G.L. (1929), 9

Approaches to beginning reading. Aukerman, R.C. (1971), 23

"Assessment in reading." Johnston, P.H. (1984), 45

The auditory and speech characteristics of poor readers. Bond, G. (1936), 65

Autobiographical material from the *History of Reading News*:

A. Sterl Artley (1998), 60

Jeanne Chall (1993, 1994), 60

Theodore Clymer (1990), 60

A. Garr Cranney (1995), 60

John Elkins (1998), 60

Grace Fernald (1998), 60

William S. Gray (1985), 60

Albert Harris (1991), 60

Nancy Larrick (1996), 60

Walter MacGinitie (1991), 60

Olive Niles (1992), 60

Sidney Rauch (1998), 60

H.A. Robinson (1997), 60

Helen M. Robinson (1988), 60

Nila B. Smith (1977), 60

Ralph Staiger (1988, 1989), 60

B

"The basal reader in American reading instruction." Hoffman, J.V., & Roser, N. (1987), 48

A basic sight vocabulary. Dolch, E. (1936), 32

Basic sight vocabulary cards test. Dolch, E.W. (1926), 46

Beginning to read. Adams, M.J. (1990), 23

Bibliography on the problems related to the analysis, prevention, and correction of reading difficulties. Betts, E.A. (1934), 17

Bibliography relating to reading on the high school and college level. Strang, R. (1939), 20

Books and reading or what books shall I read or how should I read them. Porter, N. (1870), 13

Broken promises: Reading instruction in twentieth-century in America. Shannon, P. (1989), 49

C

Children learn to read. Russell, D.H. (1949), 49

Children who cannot read. Monroe, M. (1932), 42

Children who read early. Durkin, D. (1966), 38

"Classroom assessment of reading." Calfee, R., & Hiebert, E. (1991), 45

Classroom reading and the work of Arthur Gates: 1921–1930. Vance, E. (1985), 59

"Cloze procedure: A new tool for measuring readability." Taylor, W.L. (1953), 36

"The cloze procedure revisited." Rankin, E.F. (1974), 35

"Colonial Francis Parker and beginning reading instruction." Kline, E., Moore, D.W., & Moore, S. (1987), 57

A common heritage: Noah Webster's blue-back speller. Monaghan, E.J. (1983), 49

Comparative studies of current practice in reading, with techniques for the improvement of teaching. Zirbes, L. (1927), 67

The composing processes of twelfth graders. Emig, J. (1971), 62

Considering the meaning. Leonard, J.P., & Salisbury, R. (1941), 54

"Conversations: Values of literacy history." Moore, D., Monaghan, E.J., & Hartman, D. (1997), 12

D

The development and application of criteria for appraising reading programs in elementary schools. Allen, R.V. (1948), 64

Diagnostic and remedial teaching. Brueckner, L.J., & Melby, E.O. (1931), 53

Dick and Jane go to church: A history of the Cathedral Readers. Spiker, T.M. (1997), 50

Durrell analysis of reading difficulty. Durrell, D. (1932), 46

E

"Early reading from a developmental perspective." Mason, J.M. (1984), 38

Early textbooks of English: A guide. Michael, I. (1993), 48

The effect of a single reading on the retention of various types of material in the content subjects of the elementary school curriculum as measured by immediate and delayed recall. Yoakam, G. (1922), 67

"The effect of kinaesthetic factors in the development of word recognition in the case of non-readers." Fernald, G., & Keller, H. (1921), 41

Effective reading instruction in the elementary school. Broom, M.E., Duncan, M.A., Emig, D., & Stuber, J. (1942), 53

The elements of pedagogy. White, E.E. (1886), 56

Elocution and reading. Brooks, E. (1885), 53

"Emergent literacy." Sulzby, E., & Teal, W. (1991), 39

"Essai sur la physilolgie de la lecture." Javal, E. (1879) [listed under Huey, 1908], 10

Essentials of teaching reading. Sherman, E.B., & Reed, A.A. (1909), 55

"Examination of a recent criticism of non-oral beginning reading." McDade, J.E. (1944), 29

An experimental appraisal of certain techniques for the study of oral composition. Betts, E. (1931), 65

An experimental study of the eye-voice span in reading. Buswell, G.T. (1922), 45, 65

"An experimental study of visual fixation." Dodge, R. (1907) [listed under Huey, 1908], 10

"An historical exploration of content area reading instruction." Moore, D.W., Readence, J.E., & Rickelman, R.J. (1983), 13

F

Factors associated with the reading achievement of children from a migratory population. Huus, H. (1944), 66

Factors underlying major reading disabilities at the college level. Holmes, J.A. (1949), 66

The first R: The Harvard report on reading in elementary schools. Austin, M.C., & Morrison, C. (1963), 8

Foundations of reading instruction. Betts, E.A. (1946), 52

Fundamental factors of comprehension in reading. Davis, F.B. (1950), 65

Further studies in the history of reading. Brooks, G. (1993), 17

G

Gates reading survey test. Gates, A.I. (1931), 46

Growing into reading. Monroe, M. (1951), 54

GYNS AT WK: A child learns to write and read. Bissex, G. (1980), 61

H

Handbook for remedial reading. Kottmeyer, W. (1947), 54

Handbook of reading research. Pearson, P.D. et al. (1984), 16, 19, 31, 38, 46

Handbook of reading research: Volume II. Barr, R. et al. (1991), 16, 39, 45

Handbook of reading research: Volume III. Kamil, M.L. et al. (2000), 18, 45

"A history of college reading." Stahl, N.A., & King, J.R. (2000), 19

A history of reading. Manguel, A. (1996), 11

"The history of reading research." Venezky, R.L. (1984), 19, 31, 46

"History of reading: Status and sources of a growing field." Cranney, A.G., & Miller, J. (1987), 9

A historical analysis of American reading instruction. Smith, N.B. (1935), 67

"An historical exploration of content area reading instruction." Moore, D.W., Readence, J. E., & Rickelman, R.J. (1983), 13

How to become a better reader. Witty, P. (1953), 56

How to increase reading ability: A guide to diagnostic and remedial methods. Harris, A.J. (1940), 42

How to make type readable. Patterson, D.G., & Tinker, M. (1940), 35

How to read. Kerfoot, J.B. (1916), 11

How to read a book: The art of getting a liberal education. Adler, M.J. (1940), 7

How to teach reading. Pennell, M.E., & Cusak, A.M. (1924), 55

How to teach reading in the public schools. Clark, S.H. (1898), 53

How to teach your baby to read: The gentle revolution. Doman, G. (1963), 37

I

Improvement of basic reading abilities. Durrell, D.D. (1940), 53

The improvement of reading. Cole, L. (1938), 24

The improvement of reading. Gates, A.I. (1927), 42

An index to professional literature on reading and related topics. Betts, E.A., & Betts, T.M. (1945), 17

Individualizing your reading program. Veatch, J. (1959), 26

The influence of reading ability on the validity of group intelligence tests. (Dissertation). Clymer, T. (1952), 65

The initial teaching alphabet. Downing, J.A. (1962), 25

The initial teaching alphabet reading experiment. Downing, J.A. (1964), 25

"Introduction" in *History of Education Quarterly.* Kaestle, C.F. (1990), 10

An introduction to the cloze procedure. McKenna, M.C., & Robinson, R.D. (1980), 35

An investigation into the causes of severe reading retardation. Robinson, H.M. (1945), 66

L

A laboratory study of the relation of selected factors to the span of recognition in silent reading. Harris, T. (1941), 66

Language and learning. Britton, B. (1970), 61

Language in the elementary school. McKee, P. (1939), 54

"Laura Zirbes and progressive reading instruction." Moore, D. (1986), 58

Learning to read. Pitman, J. (1960), 25

Learning to read: A handbook for teachers. Carter, H.L., & McGinnis, D.J. (1953), 53

Learning to read: The great debate. Chall, J.S. (1967), 24

Lessons from a child: On the teaching and learning of writing. Calkins, L.M. (1981), 62

Literacy in the United States: Readers and reading since 1880. Kaestle, C.F., Moore, H.D., Stedman, C., Tinsley, K., & Tollinger, W.V. (1991), 10

"Literacy instruction and gender in Colonial New England." Monaghan, E.J. *(1988)*, 12

Literacy textbooks and ideology: Postwar literacy and the mythology of Dick and Jane. Luke, A. (1988), 48

M

A manual of remedial reading. Dolch, E.W. (1939), 41

The materials of reading. Uhl, W.L. (1924), 56

The measurement and improvement of silent reading at the junior-high level. Traxler, A.E. (1932), 67

The measurement of readability. Klare, G.R. (1963), 34

Memoirs From the *History of Reading News*

    A. Sterl Artley (1998), 60

    Jeanne Chall (1993, 1994), 60

    Theodore Clymer (1990), 60

    A. Garr Cranney (1995), 60

    John Elkins (1998), 60

    Grace Fernald (1998), 60

    William S. Gray (1985), 60

    Albert Harris (1991), 60

    Nancy Larrick (1996), 60

    Walter MacGinitie (1991), 60

    Olive Niles (1992), 60

    Sidney Rauch (1998), 60

    H.A. Robinson (1997), 60

    Helen M. Robinson (1988), 60

    Nila B. Smith (1977), 60

    Ralph Staiger (1988, 1989), 60

"A method for measuring the 'vocabulary burden' of textbooks." Lively, B.A., & Pressey, S.L. (1923), 35

Methods of determining readiness. Gates, A.I., Bond, G.L., & Russell, D.H. (1939), 38

"Methods of testing reading, I. Methods of testing reading, II." Gray, W.S. (1915/1916), 45

Mind in society. The development of higher psychological processes. Vygotsky, L.S. (1978), 14

N

"The necessary mental age for beginning reading." Gates, A.I. (1937), 38

New science of elocution. Hamill, S.S. (1891), 53

Non-oral reading: A study of its use in the Chicago Public Schools. Buswell, G.T. (1945), 28

Normal methods of teaching. Brooks, E. (1879), 53

O

On the psychology and physiology of reading. Huey, E. (1899), 66

On their own in reading. Gray, W.S. (1948), 25

"Oral and silent reading." Pinter, R., & Gilliland, A.R. (1916), 29

P

The philobiblon [The love of books]. Bury, R. de (1948), 8

Practice exercises and checks on silent reading in the primary grades. Zirbes, L. (1925), 56

The prevention and correction of reading disabilities. Betts, E.A. (1936), 41

A primer for readers. Tenney, E.A., & Wardle, R.M. (1942), 55

"Probable types of difficulties underlying low scores in comprehension tests." Hilliard, G.E. (1924), 32

Problems in the improvement of reading in high school and college. Strang, R., & Rose, F.C. (1938), 55

Problems in the psychology of reading. Quartz, J.O. (1897), 30, 32

Procedures used in selecting textbooks. Whipple, G. (1936), 67

"Progress in the study of readability." Gray, W.S. (1937), 34

Psychology and pedagogy of reading. Huey, E. (1908)1, 9

The psychology and teaching of reading. Schonell, F.J. (1945), 55

Psychology of reading. Dearborn, W. (1905), 65

The psychology of reading: An experimental study of the reading process and eye movements. Dearborn, W.F. (1906) [listed under Huey, 1908], 10

The psychology of teaching reading. Anderson, I.H., & Dearborn, W.F. (1952), 23

R

Read and comprehend. Knight, P.E., & Traxler, A.E. (1937), 54

"The reader, the scribe, the thinker: A critical look at the history of American reading and writing instruction." Monaghan, E.J., & Saul, E.W. (1987), 12

"Reading: A psycholinguistic guessing game." Goodman, K. (1967), 25

Reading activities in the primary grades. Storm, G.E., & Smith, N.B. (1930), 55

SUBJECT INDEX

26, 44
Parker, Colonial Francis, 57
Pedagogy of reading, 1, 9, 52, 53, 54, 55, 56
Phonics, 23, 24, 47
Politics and reading12, 49
Primers, American, 50
Professional references and reading, 17, 52, 53, 54, 55, 56
Progressive reading instruction, 58
Psycholinguistics and reading, 25–26
Psychology of reading, 1, 9, 10, 14, 23, 30, 32, 55, 65, 66

R

Rauch, Sidney, 60
Readability, 34, 35, 36
Readers in the United States, 10, 58
Readiness, 37, 38, 39, 54
Reading and writing, 9, 12
Reading educators, 8, 34, 37, 47, 57, 58, 59, 60, 68
Reading instruction, 10, 11, 12, 13, 14, 17, 18, 19, 20, 21, 23, 26, 27, 29, 30, 38, 40, 47, 48, 49, 50, 52, 53, 57, 58, 59, 67
Remediation, see disabilities in reading
Research, summaries of reading, 16, 18, 31, 40, 46
Robinson, H. Alan, 19, 32, 50, 60, 69
Robinson, Helen, 18, 38, 43, 60, 66, 69

S

Silent reading, 9, 14, 28, 29, 30, 32, 46, 56, 66, 67

Smith, Nila B., 19, 50, 55, 60, 67
Society for the History of Authorship, Reading and Publishing, 70
Speed reading, 15
Staiger, Ralph, 60

T

Teachers of reading, professional references in this discipline, 8, 52, 53, 54, 55, 56
Testing reading, see assessment in reading
Tests of reading, 45, 46
Textbook Colloquium, 71
Textbooks for reading instruction, 35, 42, 48, 49, 67
Thorndike, Edward, 31, 32, 33, 35

V

Values in studying literacy history, 5, 12, 13
Vocabulary, 31, 32, 33, 35, 46

W

Webster, Noah, 49
Word lists, 32, 35
Word recognition, 22, 23, 25, 41, 44
Writing, 2, 4, 7, 9, 12, 14, 15, 24, 61, 62, 63, 70
Writing systems, 24, 62

Y

Yearbooks, reading, 19, 68, 69, 70
Yoakum, Gerald, 30

Z

Zirbes, Laura, 56, 58, 67